EAST ANGLIA FROM ABOVE

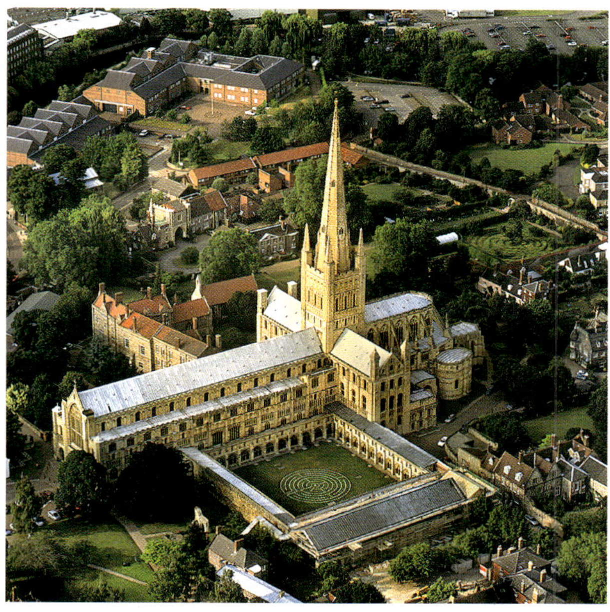

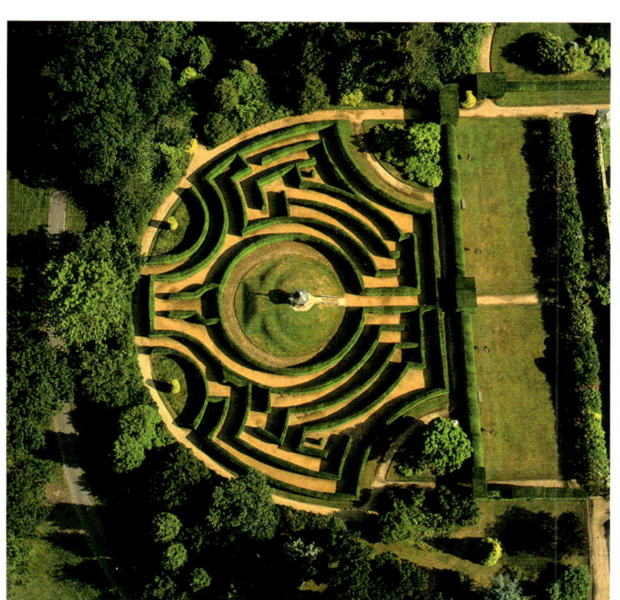

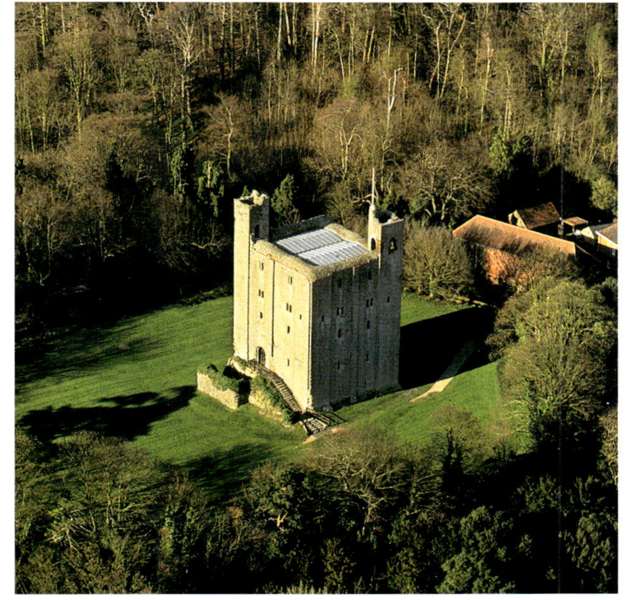

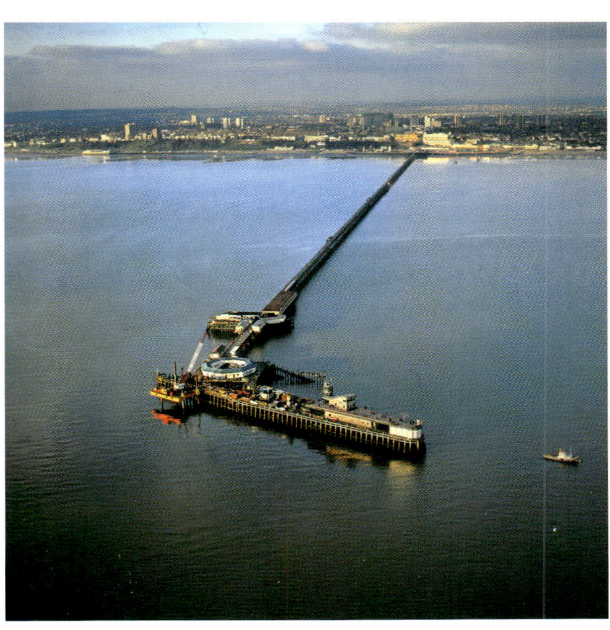

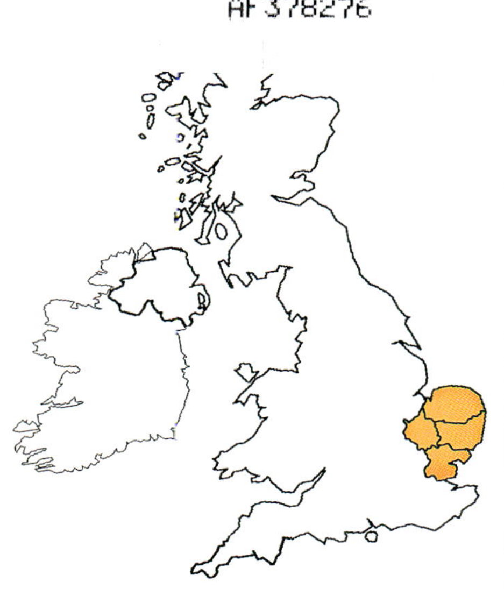

Contents

Introduction

Magnificent country estates, castles, windmills, fields of lavender and endless sandy beaches: this is East Anglia, made up of Norfolk, Suffolk, Cambridgeshire, and Essex. Before the Romans and Anglo-Saxons this was the land of Queen Boudicca and the Iceni. Angliae, North Folk, South Folk, and the Isle of Eels: place names evocative of the past. At the time of the Norman conquest, East Anglia was the most densely populated area of Britain. Today, the picturesque market towns and villages can still trace their history back to Saxon times and beyond. The landscape was very different then: at least until the Middle Ages, it was densely forested with oak, but was gradually cleared for ship and house building, and wheat farming.

To the south there is Essex, between the rivers Thames and Stour. Here, Epping Forest is the last fragment of the great Waltham Forest. Essex was the centre of Roman occupation, with Colchester their chosen capital. Helped by its close proximity to London, the county has the fastest population growth anywhere in Britain.

North of the river Stour is Suffolk. Here is peace and tranquillity and the essence of rural England captured on oil and canvas by Gainsborough and Constable who painted many famous works here, the locations of which can still be recognised.

Inland is Cambridgeshire and areas of uplands, or "isles" such as the Isle of Ely, in an otherwise rather flat landscape. The ancient industries of basket and paper-making have largely given way to fields of cereal crops. The county is dominated by Cambridge with its fine architecture and world famous university.

Norfolk is the biggest and least populated county in East Anglia. Norwich is its cathedral city and cultural centre. Here are the famous Norfolk Broads, a popular holiday destination among boating enthusiasts during summer months, though bleak and windswept during winter. Further north, on the fringe of the Wash, are the Fens: low-lying marshland reclaimed in a complex of channels and sluice gates, with rivers, estuaries and mud flats which are rich havens for birds.

Photographs from top to bottom: Norwich Cathedral, Yew Hedge Maze at Somerleyton Hall, Castle Hadingham, Southend-on-Sea

Photographs, text and design by Adrian Warren and Dae Sasitorn

MYRIAD BOOKS LIMITED

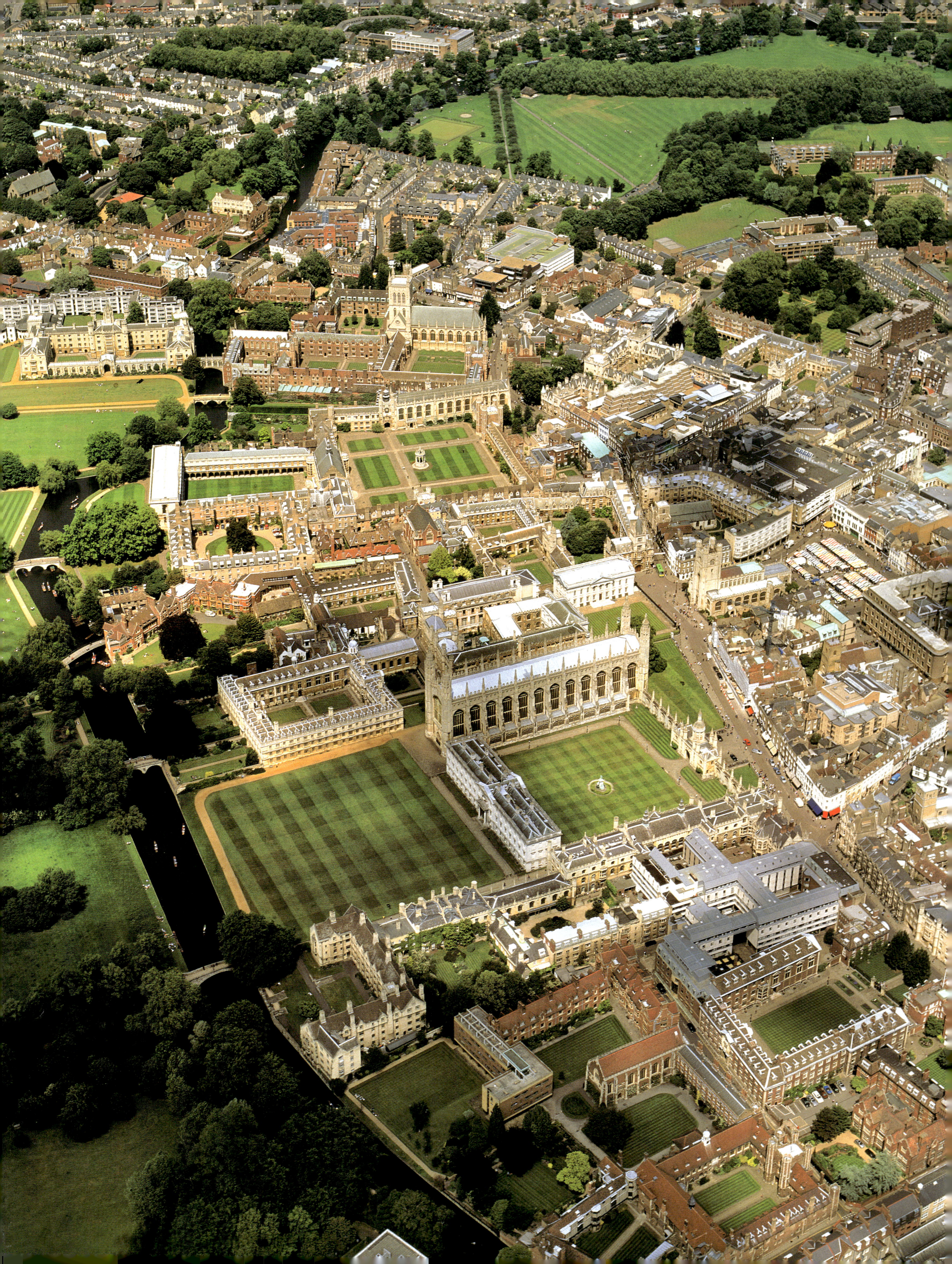

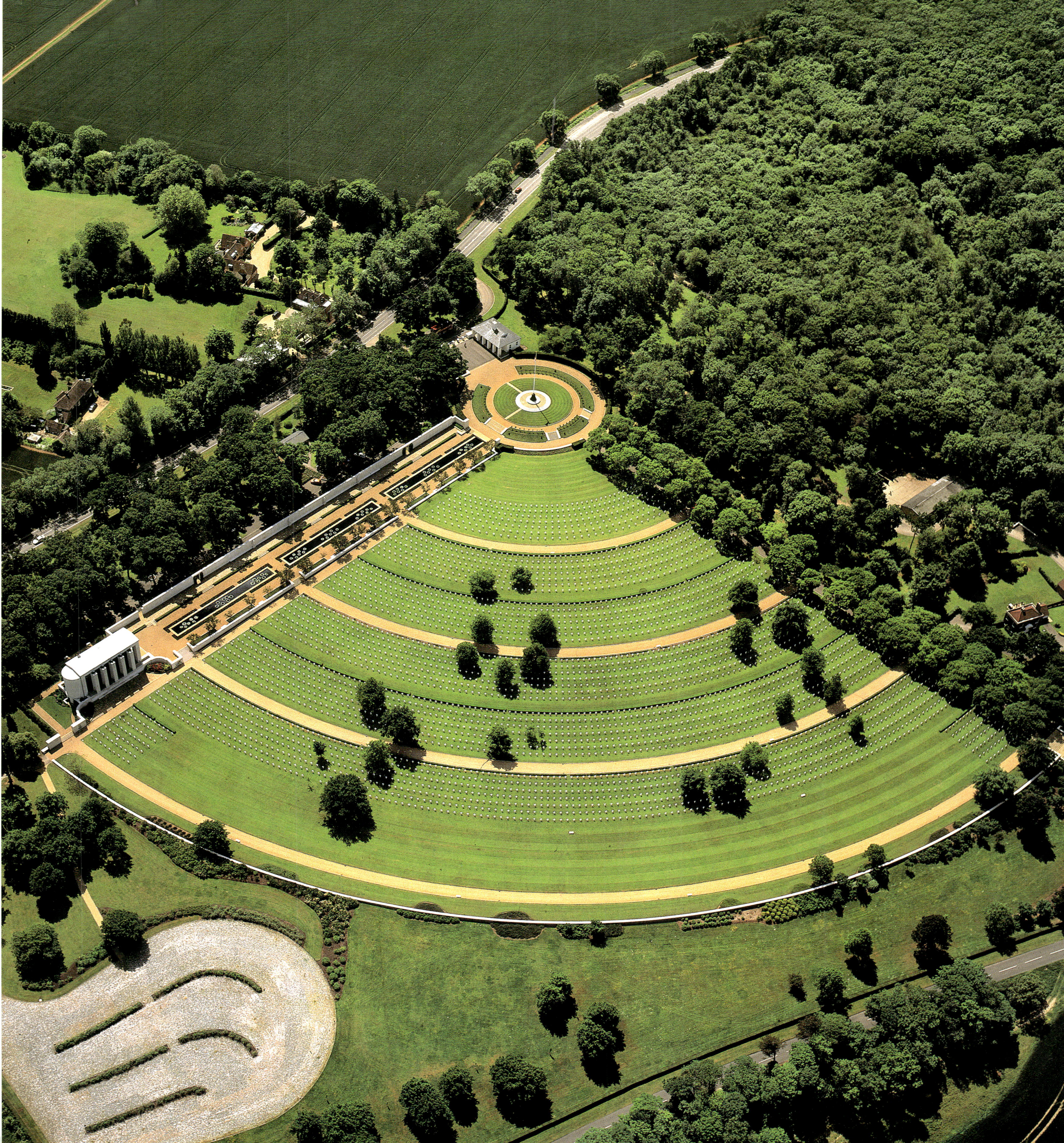

THE BEAUTIFUL CITY OF CAMBRIDGE IN CAMBRIDGESHIRE is noted for its fine architecture and is home of one of the oldest universities in the world. The photograph shows some of the colleges along the stretch of water known as the "Backs". Notable among these is King's College, founded in 1441 by Henry VI, with its famous chapel, which has the largest fan-vaulted ceiling in the world, and Trinity College, Cambridge's largest college, founded in 1546 by Henry VIII.

AMERICAN CEMETERY, MADINGLEY (ABOVE)

THE WORLD WAR II CAMBRIDGE AMERICAN CEMETERY and Memorial is located 5km (3 miles) west of Cambridge on land donated to the United States of America in honour of Americans who gave their lives during the Second World War. The 3,812 white crosses, and the Portland stone wall inscribed with 5,126 names of those whose remains were never recovered or identified, pay tribute to American servicemen and women who died in the war.

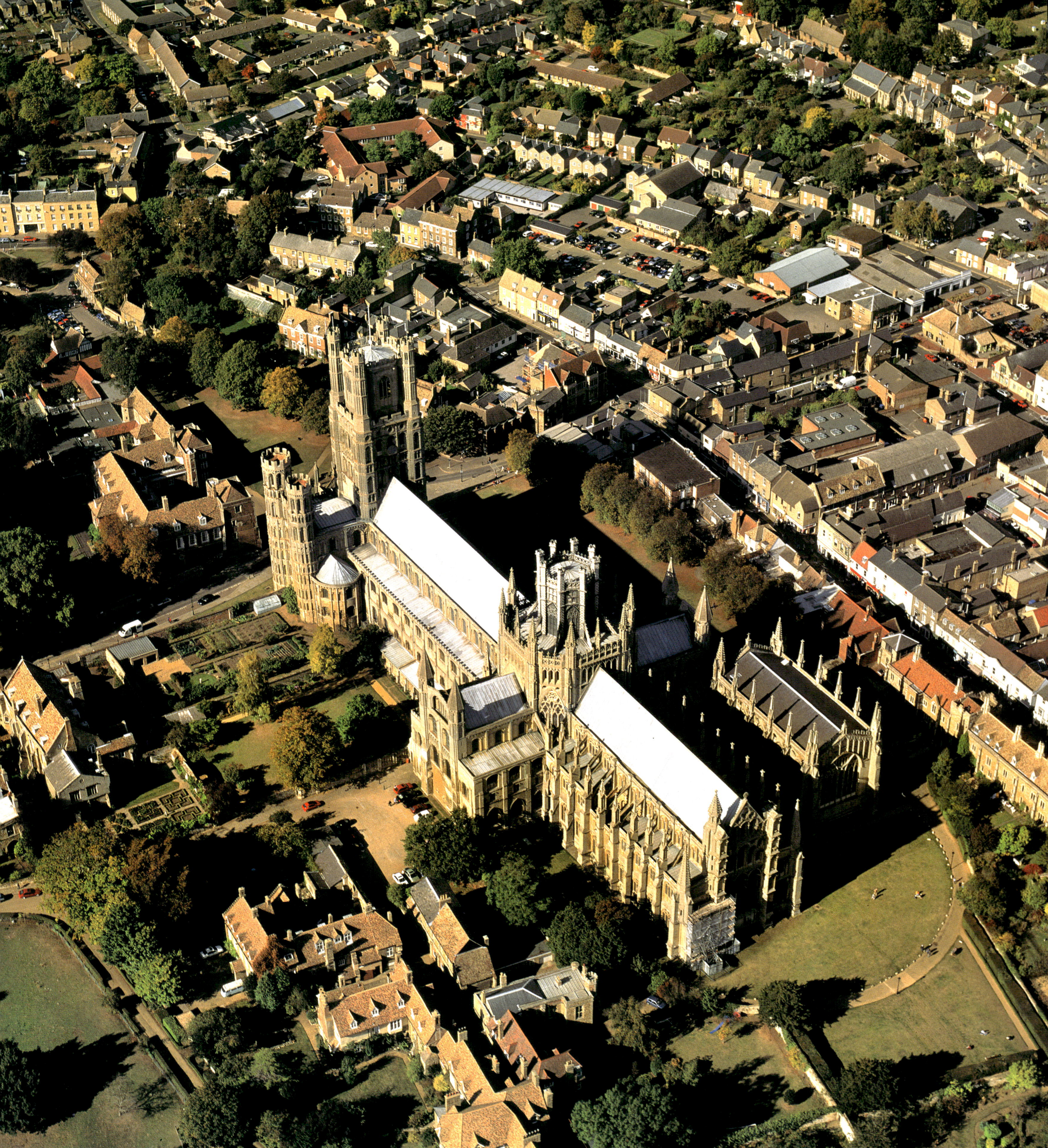

ELY CATHEDRAL (ABOVE)

ELY HAS BEEN A PLACE OF CHRISTIAN WORSHIP SINCE 673, when Etheldreda, daughter of the Anglo-Saxon King Anna, founded a convent one mile north of the Saxon village of Cratendune. Nothing survives of the Anglo-Saxon church, which was demolished to make way for the present structure, built after the Norman Conquest. In 1109 Ely became a cathedral as part of the Norman reforms of the English church.

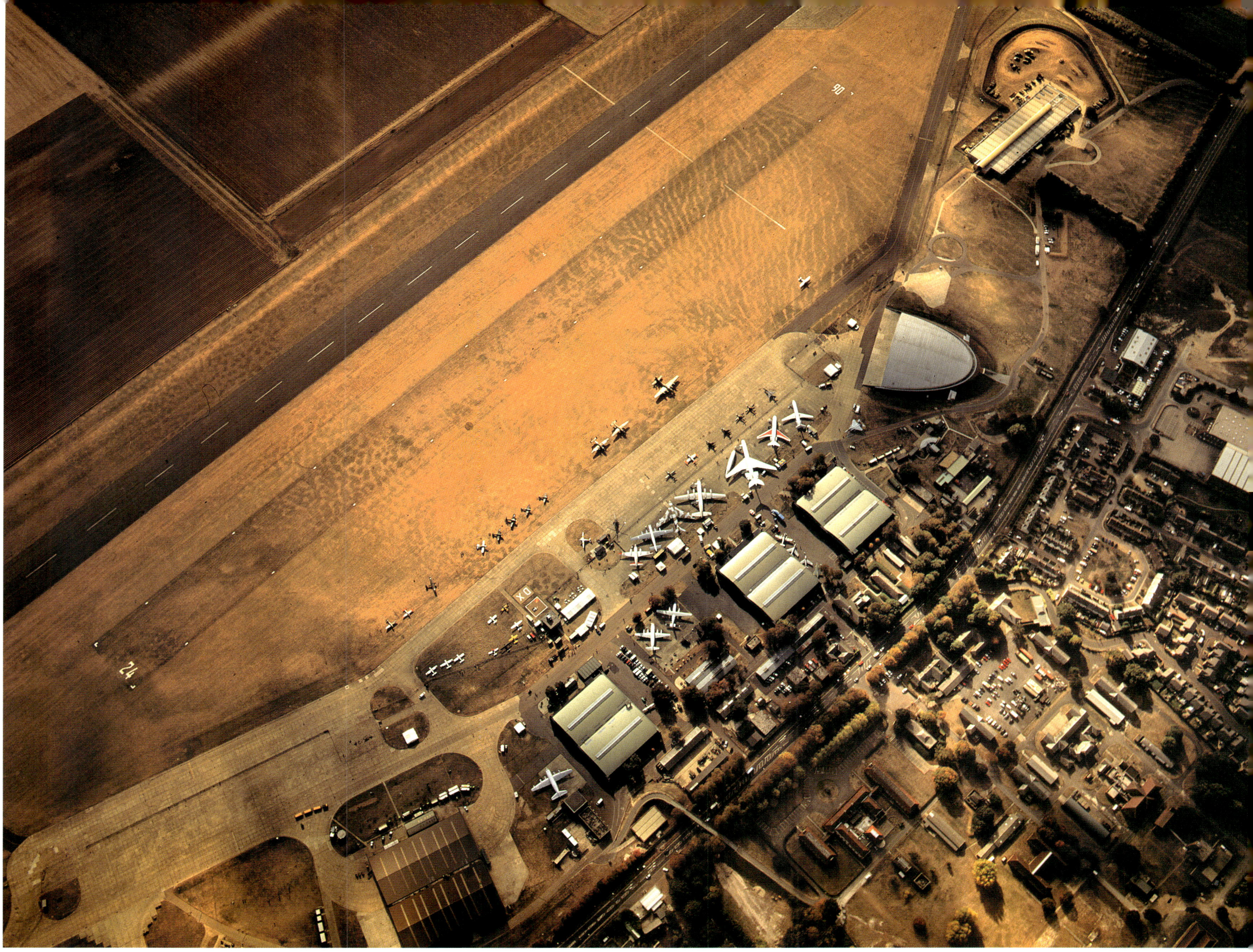

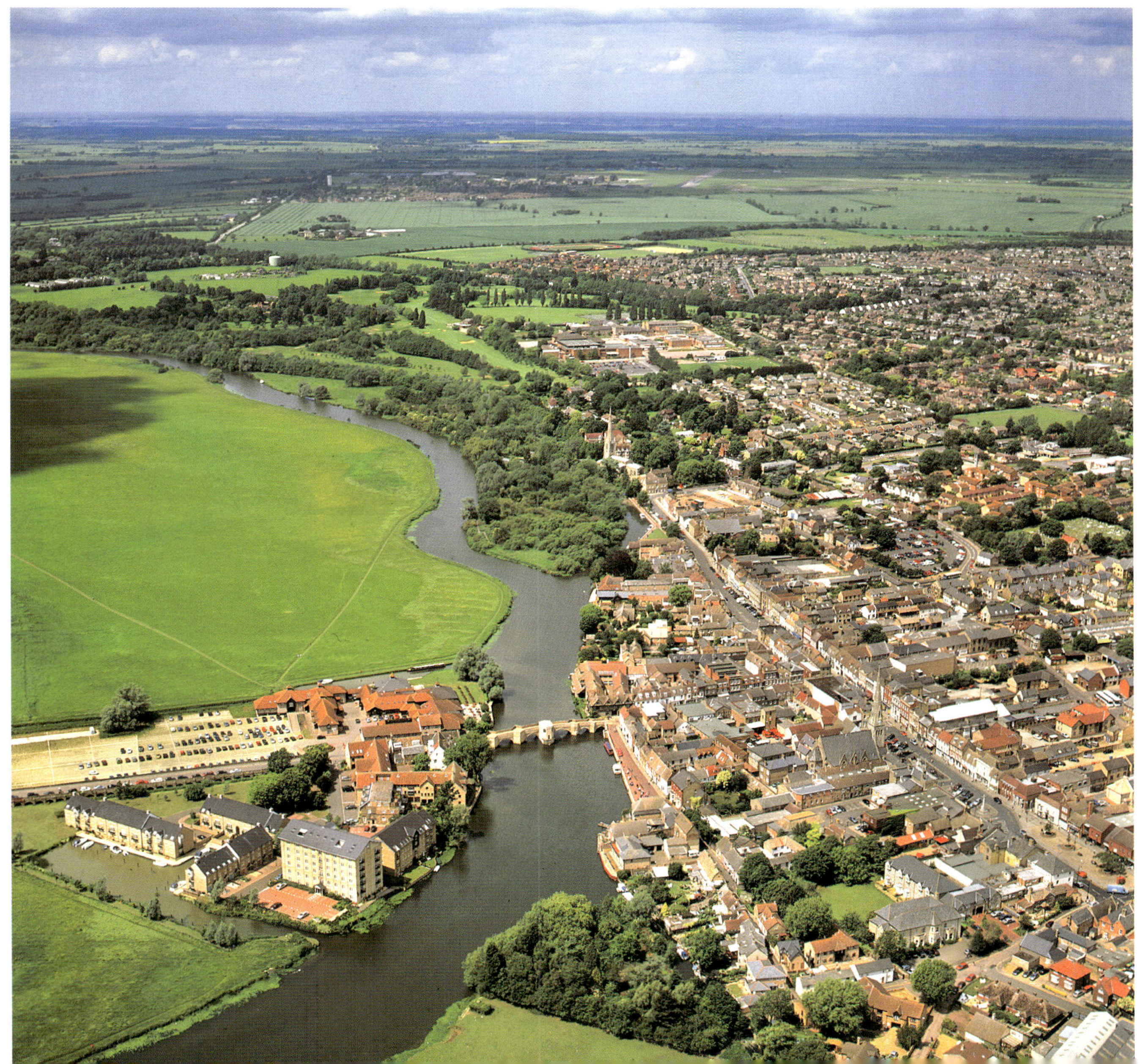

DUXFORD (ABOVE)

THE AERODROME AT DUXFORD was built during the First World War and was one of the earliest Royal Air Force stations. In August 1938 the first Spitfire was flown into Duxford by Jeffrey Quill, Supermarine's test pilot. Duxford was to become one of RAF Fighter Command's most important aerodromes in the Battle of Britain. Today Duxford is established as the European centre of aviation history. Now a branch of the Imperial War Museum, it houses outstanding collections of restored aircraft and holds regular world-renowned air shows.

ST IVES (LEFT)

THE MARKET TOWN OF ST IVES is situated on the banks of the Great Ouse, in Cambridgeshire. Nearby Huntingdon is the birthplace of Oliver Cromwell who farmed here for five years in the 1630s. St Ives has its roots in Saxon times as a small settlement called "Slepe", which is an old Saxon word meaning "muddy". Later, in medieval times, it was renowned for its fairs. The area is surrounded by flood plains and is prone to flooding. The worst floods in recent history were in 1998.

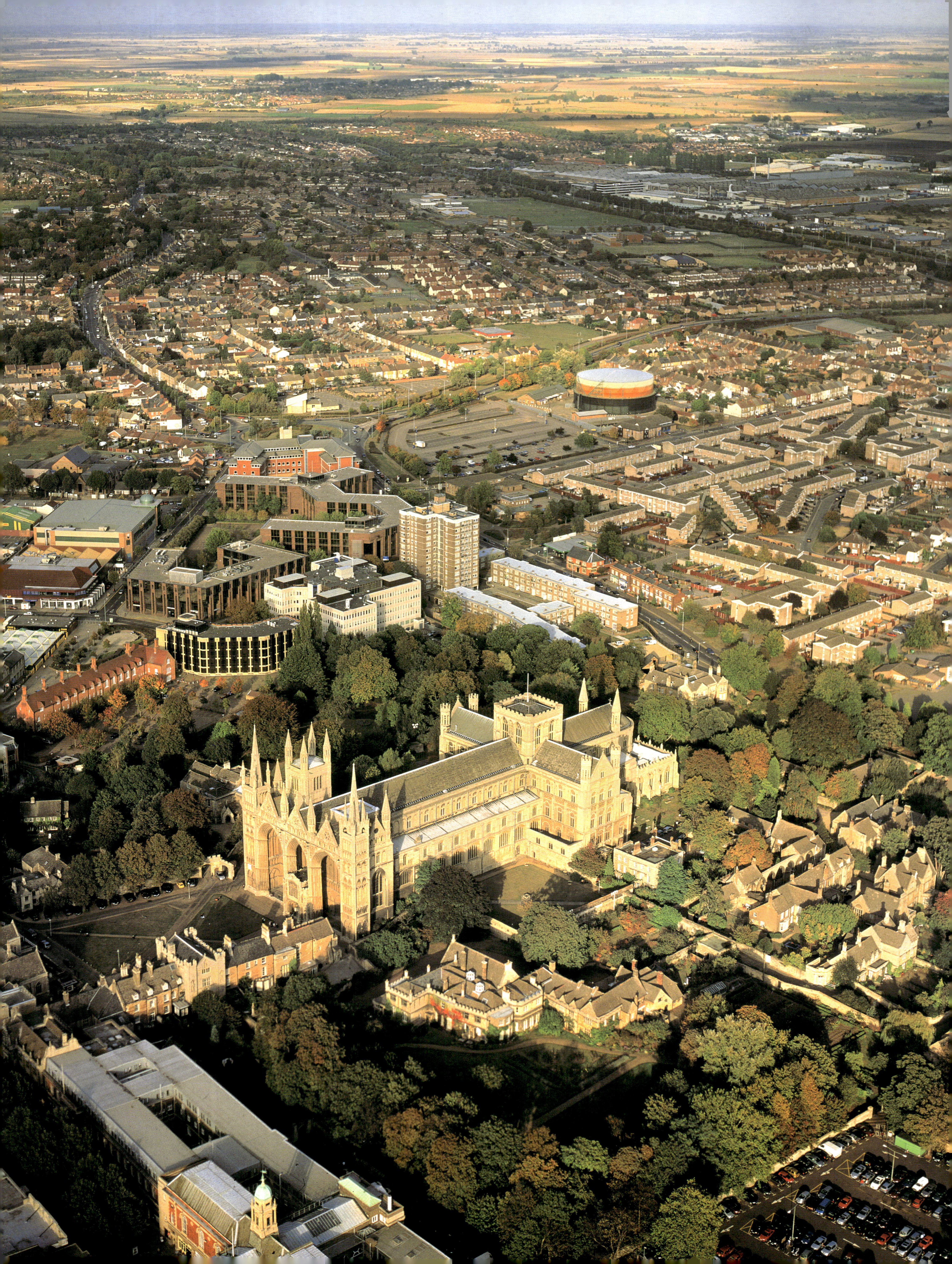

PETERBOROUGH (LEFT)

ORIGINALLY KNOWN AS MEDESHAMSTEDE,
Peterborough in Cambridgeshire has been a
centre for Christian worship for over 1,300
years. The first abbey was founded here in
655 and the present building, the Cathedral of
Peterborough, was founded in 1118 and
towers majestically over the city. The
cathedral's west front is magnificent and the
building is one of the finest examples of
Norman architecture in Europe.

THETFORD PRIORY (RIGHT)

THE PRIORY WAS FOUNDED IN 1104 by Sir
Roger Bigod, and was once the third largest in
Norfolk. Like many priories, after the
dissolution of the monasteries under Henry
VIII, the buildings fell into ruin and much of
the stone was plundered for the construction
of other buildings in the town. In Iceni and
early Saxon times, Thetford was the capital of
East Anglia, but the Normans moved
the capital to Norwich.

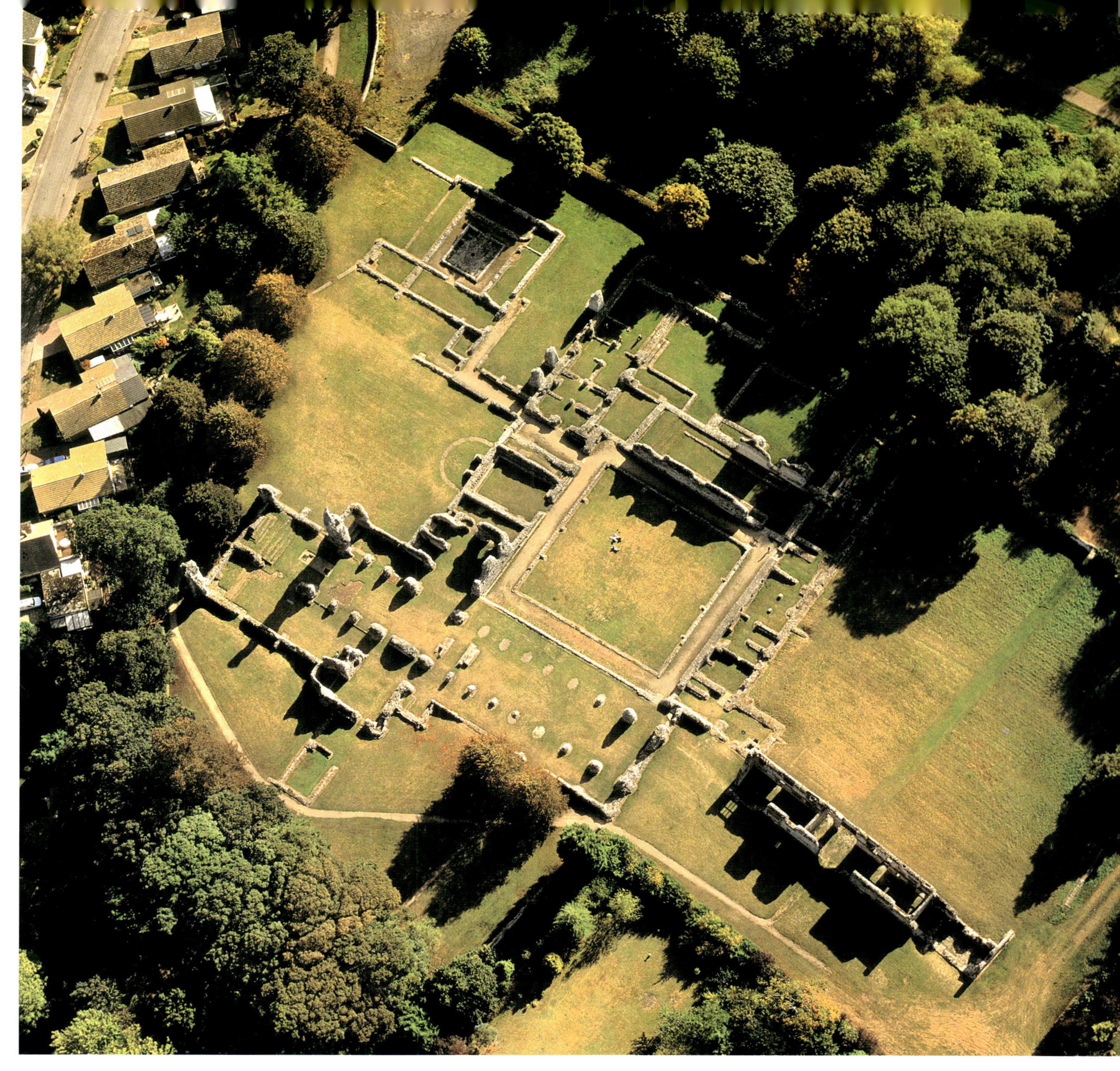

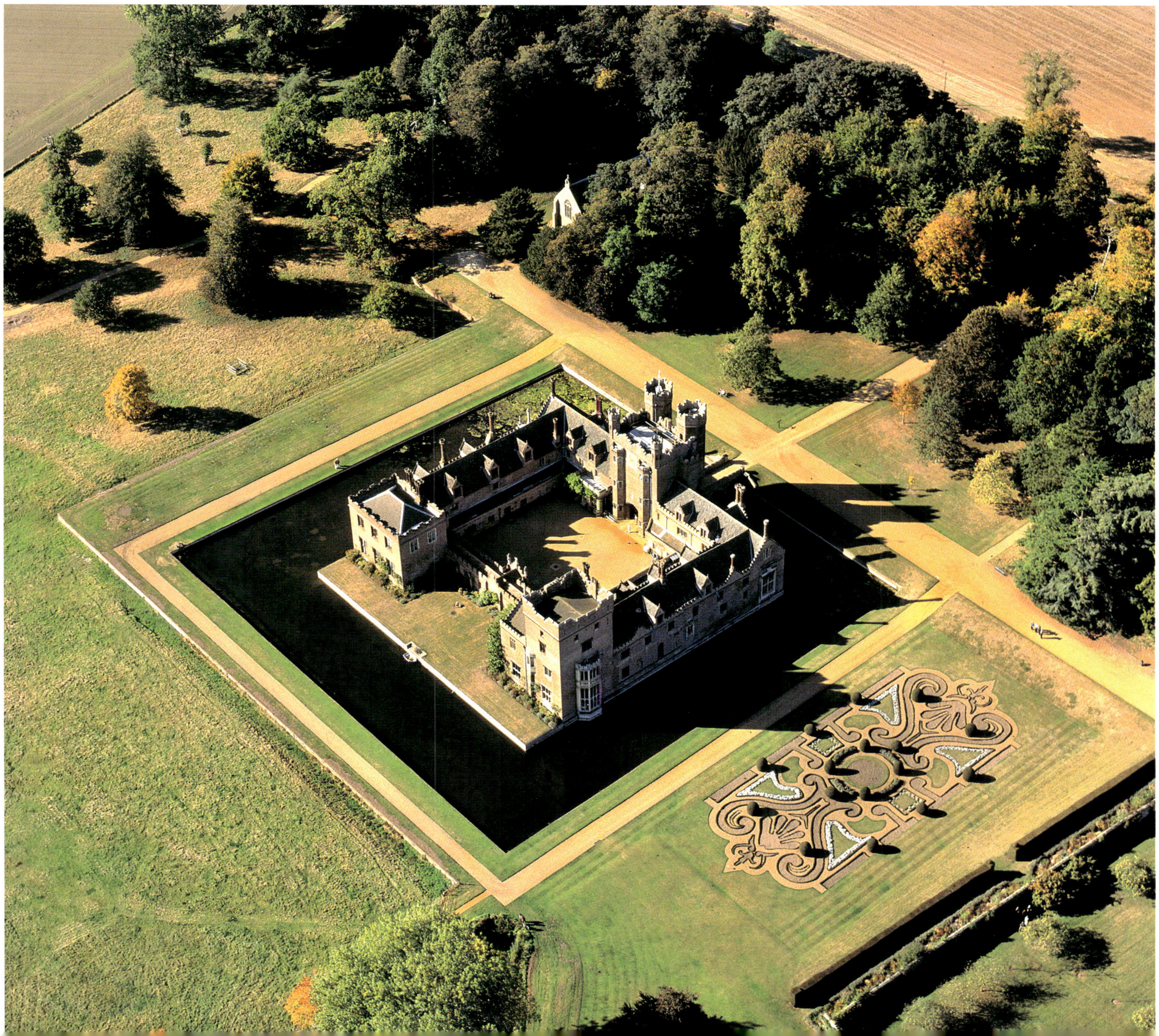

OXBURGH HALL (LEFT)

**OXBURGH HALL WAS BUILT IN
1482**, when Sir Edmund Bedingfeld
was granted a licence to
"crenellate" — or build a castle or
defensive hall — by Edward IV.
The medieval, moated manor
house was created in the style of a
castle. The original Great Hall was
demolished in 1775, and the house
was extensively restored during the
19th century. It has been the home
of the Bedingfelds since the early
15th century. Elizabeth I, under
close house arrest, visited the Hall
in 1578, in the custody of Sir
Henry Bedingfeld, who was then
Governor of the Tower of London.

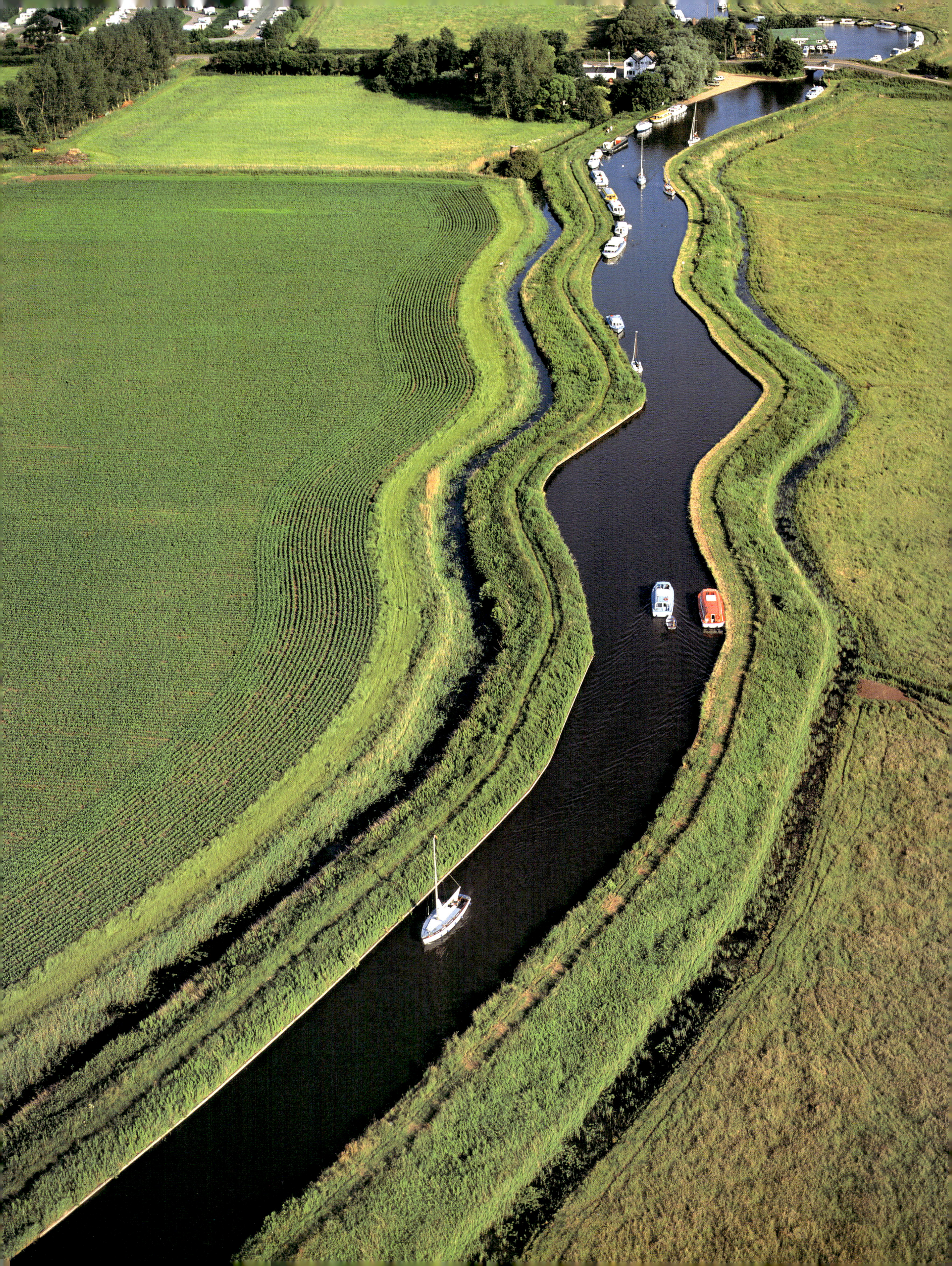

Norfolk Broads (Left)

The Broads originated in medieval times from generations of Norfolk people digging peat to use as fuel for heating and cooking. Centuries of peat removal caused deep pits to form which flooded to create lakes. Later, cuts were made to join the lakes to the rivers Ant, Bure, Thurne, Waveney and Yare creating a network of broads, meandering rivers and cut channels. The Norfolk Broads is Britain's only wetland national park. It is a haven for wildlife and a mecca for boating enthusiasts.

Cromer (Right)

A seaside resort with a church tower that is the highest in the county at 49m. Originally a small fishing village, Cromer is famous for its crabs. Coastal erosion is a continuing process here on the Norfolk coast as the North Sea waves pound the shoreline. During the Middle Ages the nearby village of Shipden was inundated and now lies some 400m out to sea. The ever-crumbling cliffs are a favourite haunt of geologists and fossil-hunters.

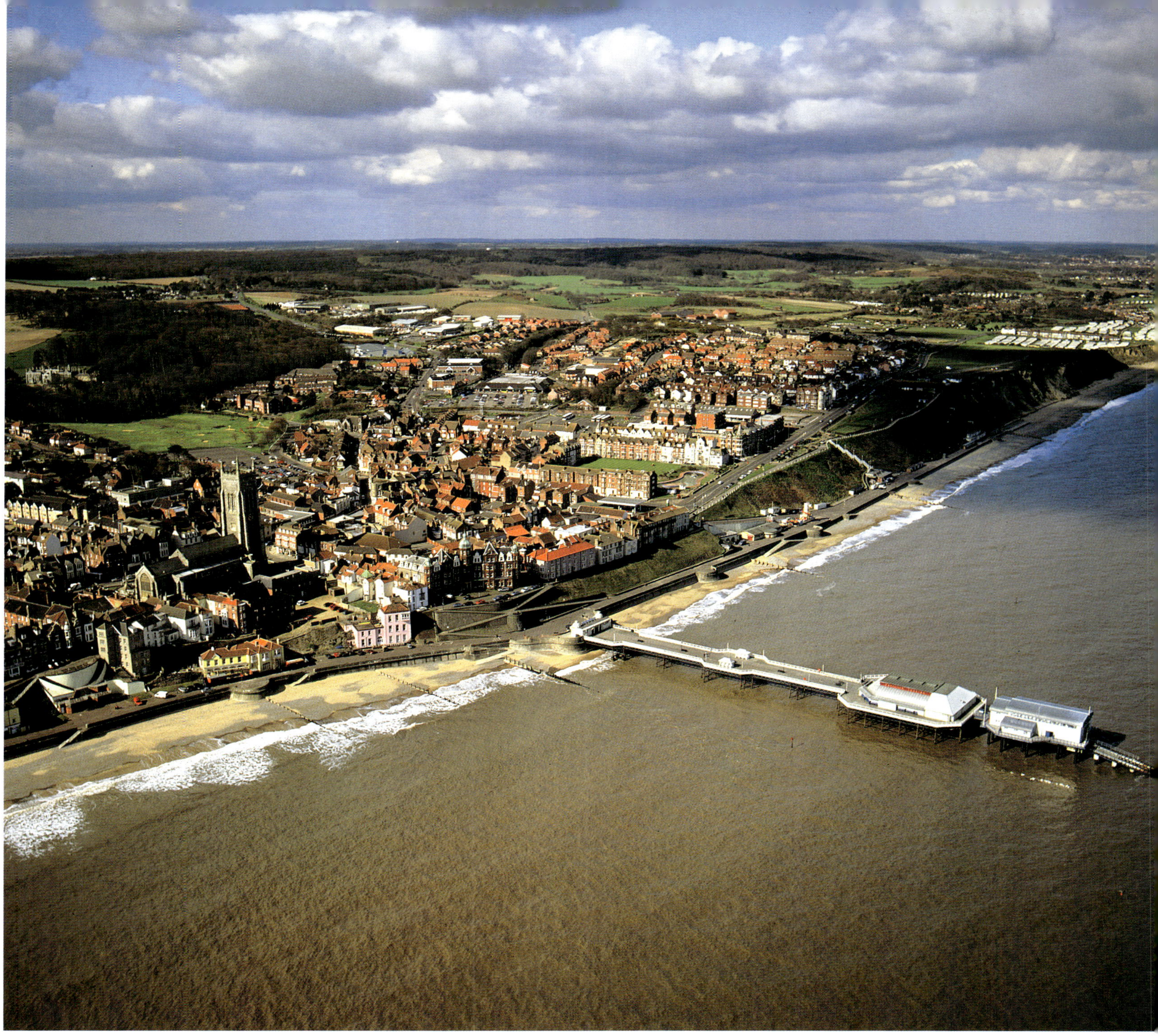

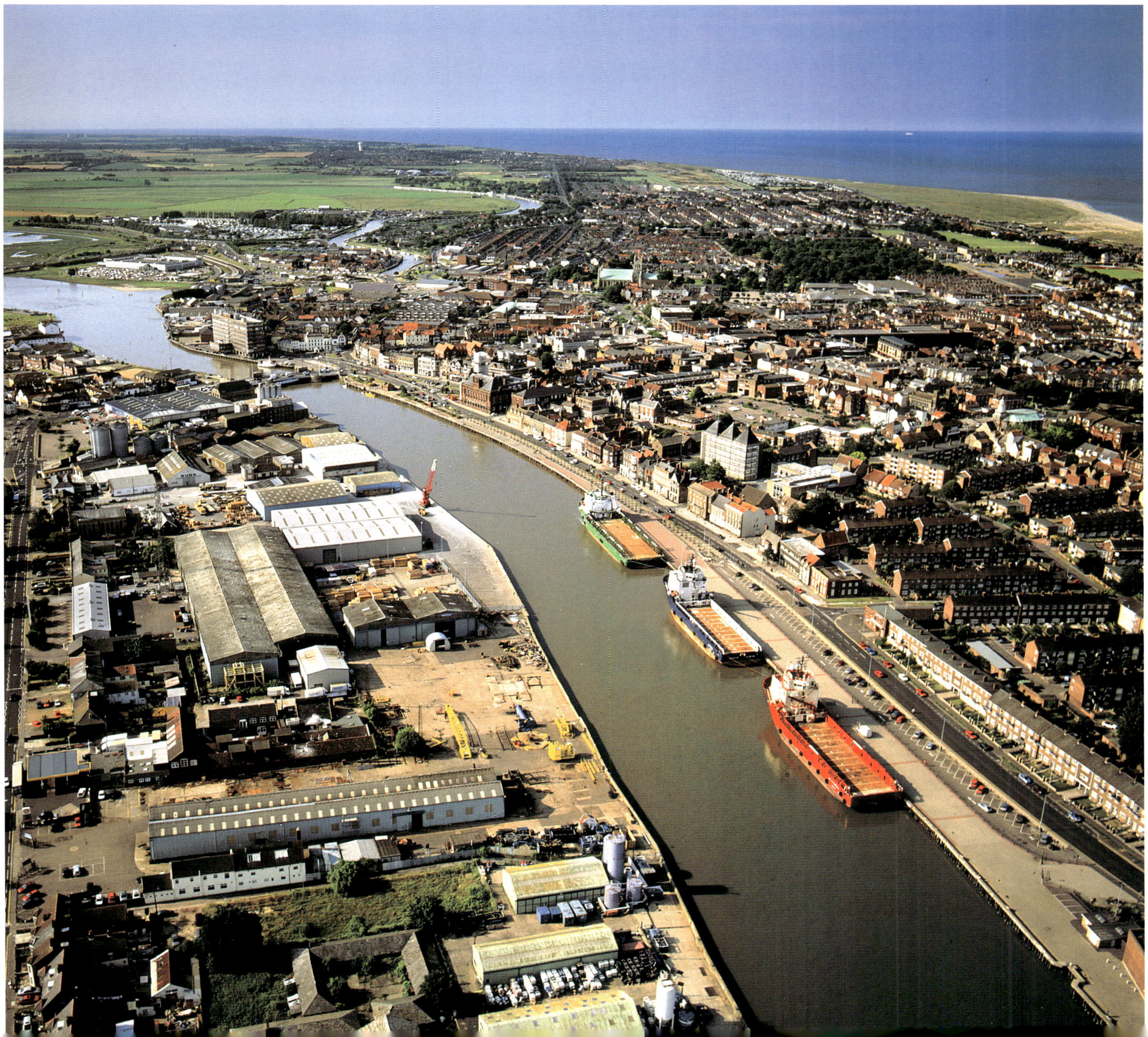

Great Yarmouth (Left)

The port of Great Yarmouth was once home for herring fishing boats. The quayside was filled with open sheds where the fish were prepared, and smokehouses produced Yarmouth kippers. Yarmouth started life during Saxon times as a small settlement on a sand bank in the estuary of the rivers Bure and Yare. Great Yarmouth is now a popular seaside holiday resort famous for its "Golden Mile", a stretch of sandy beach and leisure attractions.

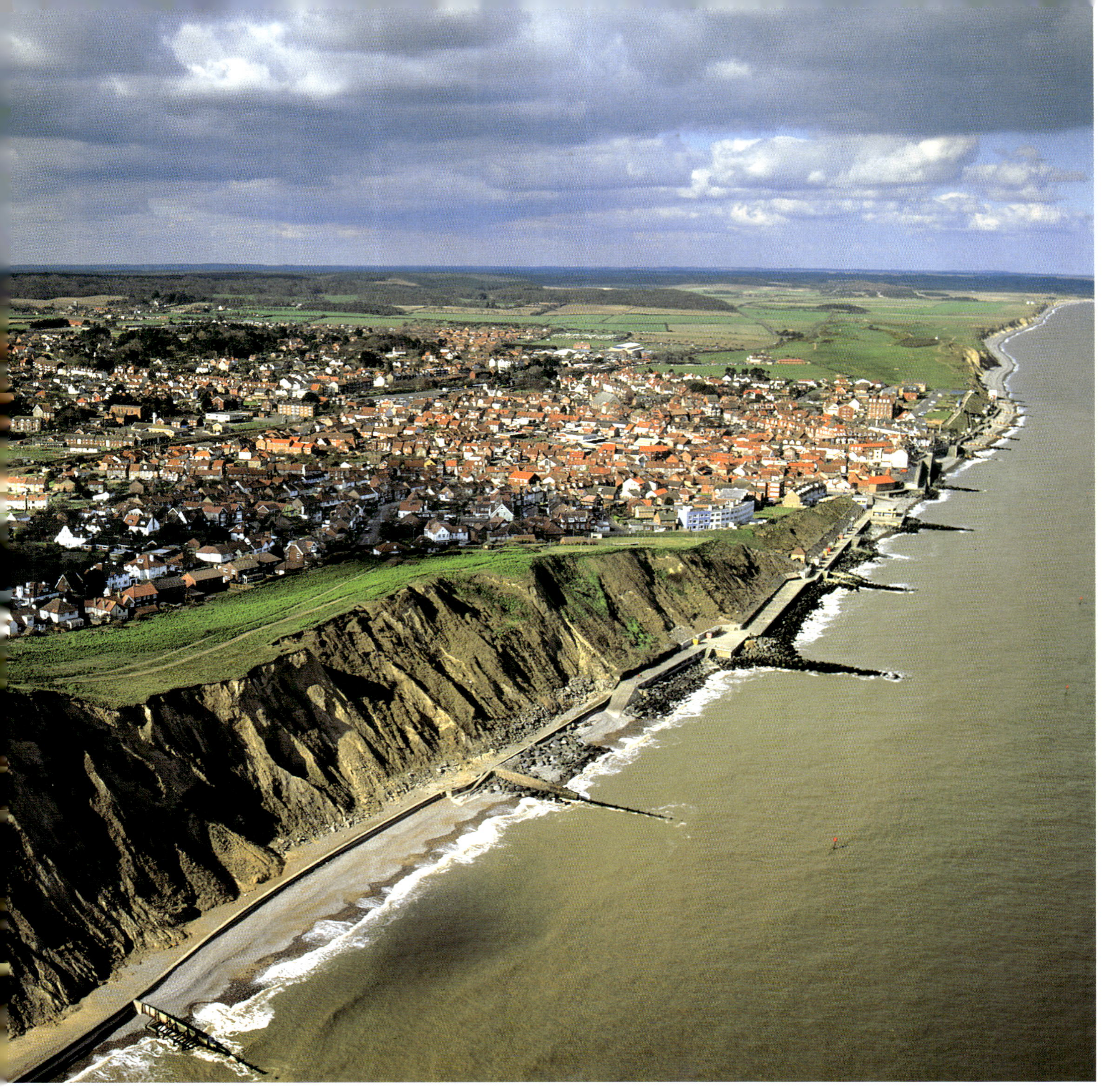

SHERINGHAM (LEFT)

SHERINGHAM IS A SEASIDE RESORT on the
Norfolk coast, with a shingle beach and sand
at low tide. Lower Sheringham is by the sea
and the ancient town, Upper Sheringham,
listed in the Domesday book of 1086, is on
the hillside above the coastal strip. As with
many of Norfolk's towns and villages, the
name is of Scandinavian origin, meaning the
"home of Scira's people".

NORWICH (RIGHT)

NORWICH IS THE CAPITAL OF NORFOLK
and is a city of churches. There are over 30
of them inside the city walls dating back to
the Middle Ages, more than in any other
western European city. Rising above them all
is the 96m tall spire of Norwich Cathedral.
Founded in 1096 as a Benedictine priory,
the Cathedral is one of the finest complete
Romanesque buildings in Europe with the
second tallest spire and the largest
monastic cloisters in England.

HUNSTANTON (RIGHT)

THIS NORFOLK COASTAL
RESORT is divided into the
village of Old Hunstanton and
the newer resort town of
Hunstanton St Edmund. The
village and the lands surrounding
it were given by William the
Conqueror to the Le Strange
family who remained Lords of
the Manor for over 800 years.
Interesting fossils have been
discovered in the cliffs here: the
top layer of the cliff is white
chalk from the Upper
Cretaceous era but beneath it is
a band of red chalk limestone
from over 15 million years ago.
In January 1953 the worst
floods on record hit the Norfolk
coast and many people
lost their lives.

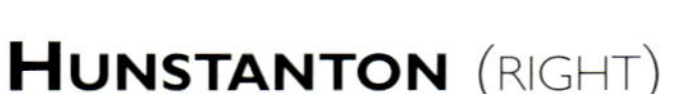

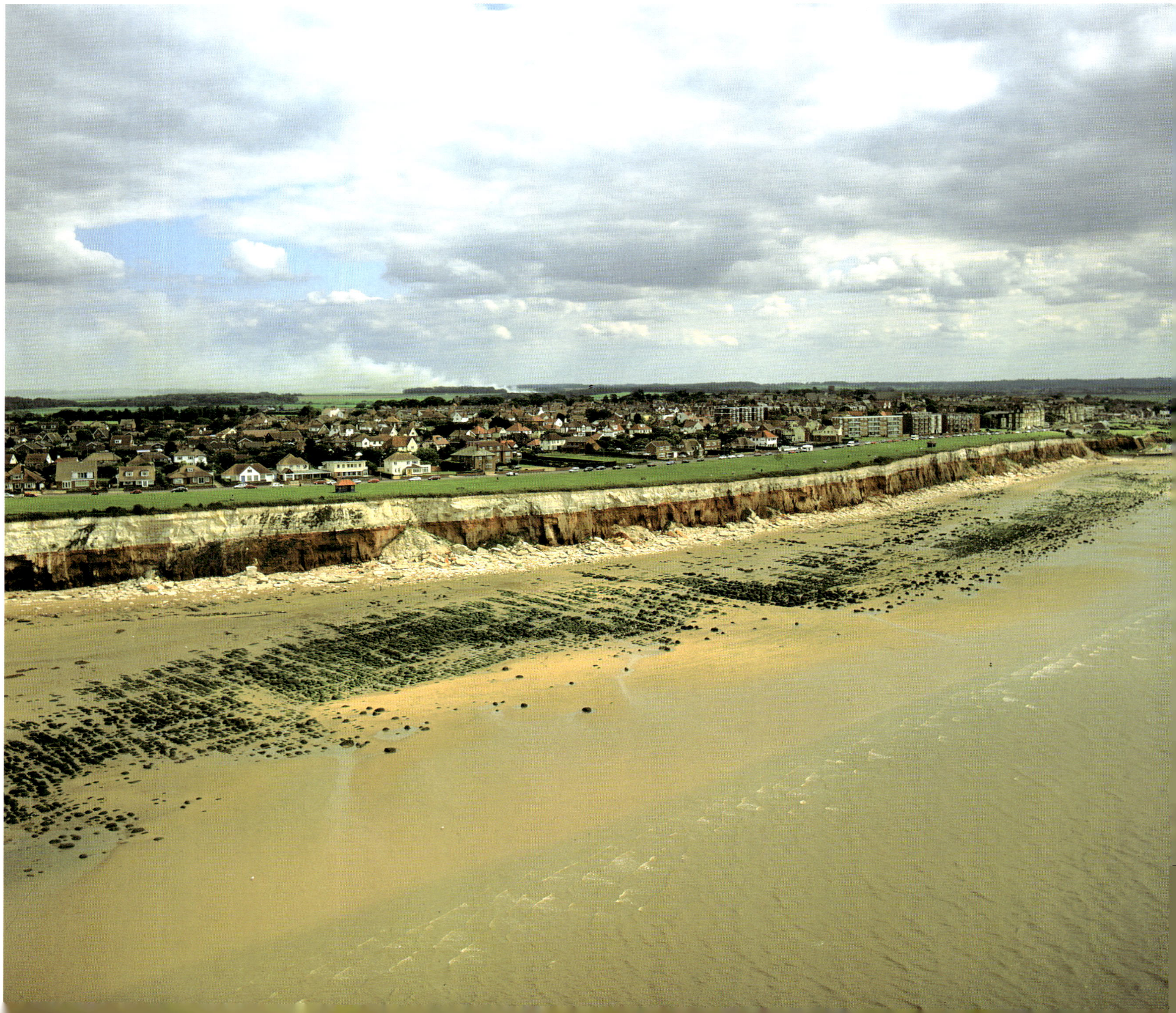

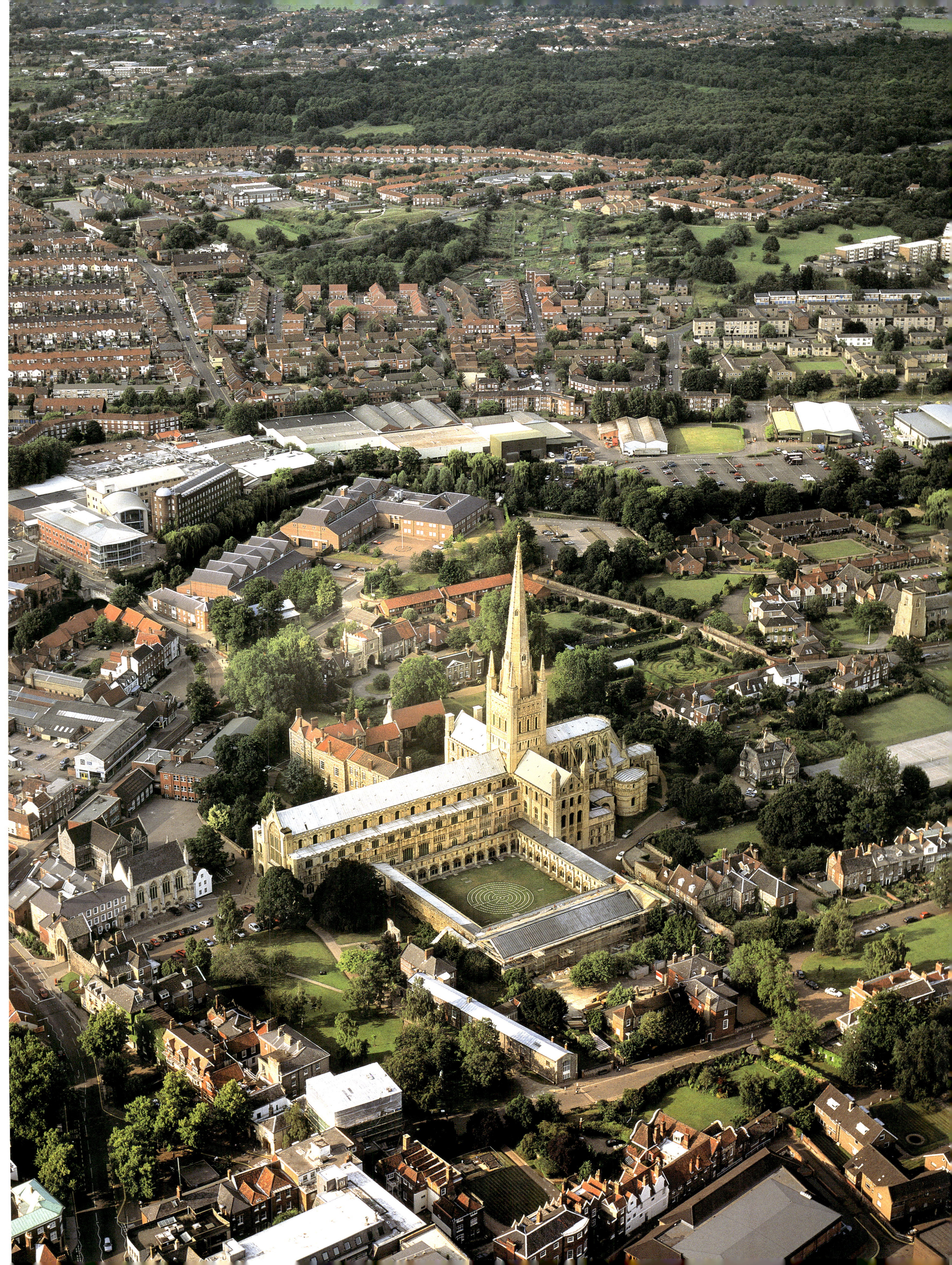

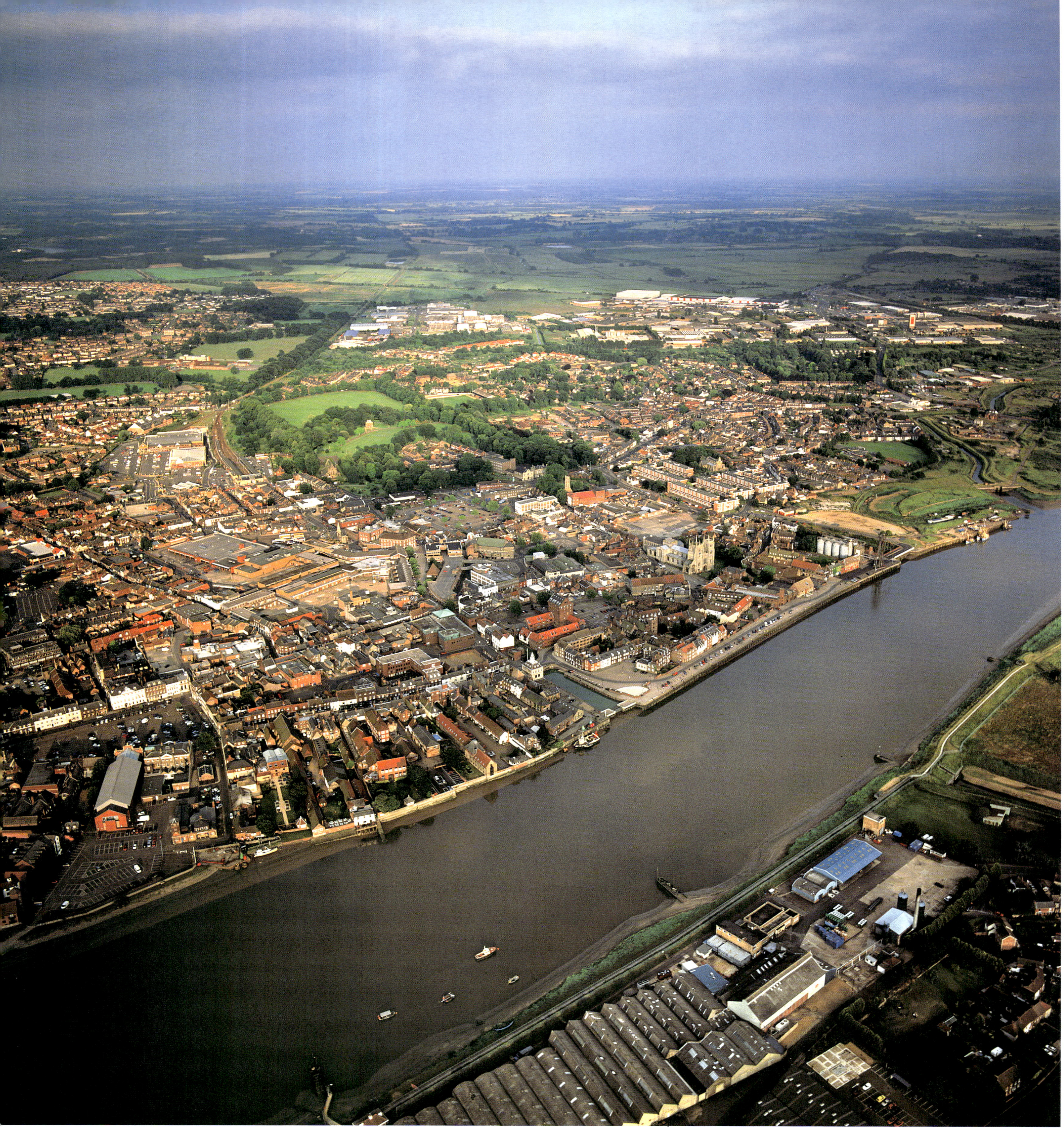

KING'S LYNN (ABOVE)

KING'S LYNN, FORMERLY BISHOP'S LYNN before it became royal property, is a commercially historic town situated on the River Ouse as it meanders towards the Wash. It became an important port for trade in wool, cloth and agricultural products in medieval times. The old town walls, traces of which can still be seen, show how the town has grown. Among the traditional seafaring community was a local man called George Vancouver who explored north-west America.

BLAKENEY POINT (RIGHT)

AN EXTENSIVE NETWORK OF MARSHY CREEKS meet at Blakeney Point. A vast spit of shingle and sand with sand dunes, salt marshes and mud flats on the landward side, protected from all but the very highest tides, has formed a natural wildlife sanctuary: seals bask on sandbanks; some 263 different species of birds have been recorded here, of which at least 33 breed; and the plant life is also extensive. The area was acquired by the National Trust in 1912.

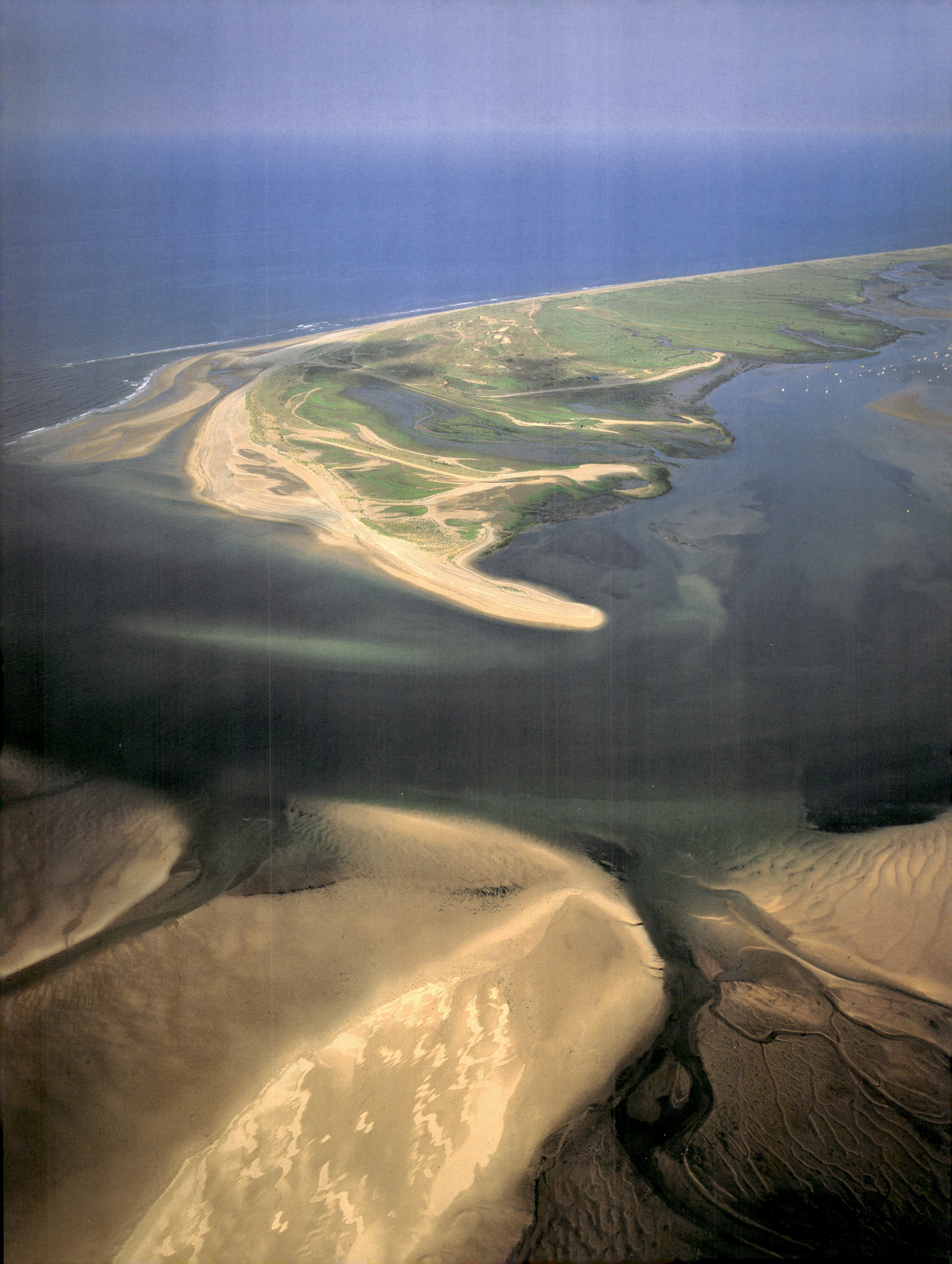

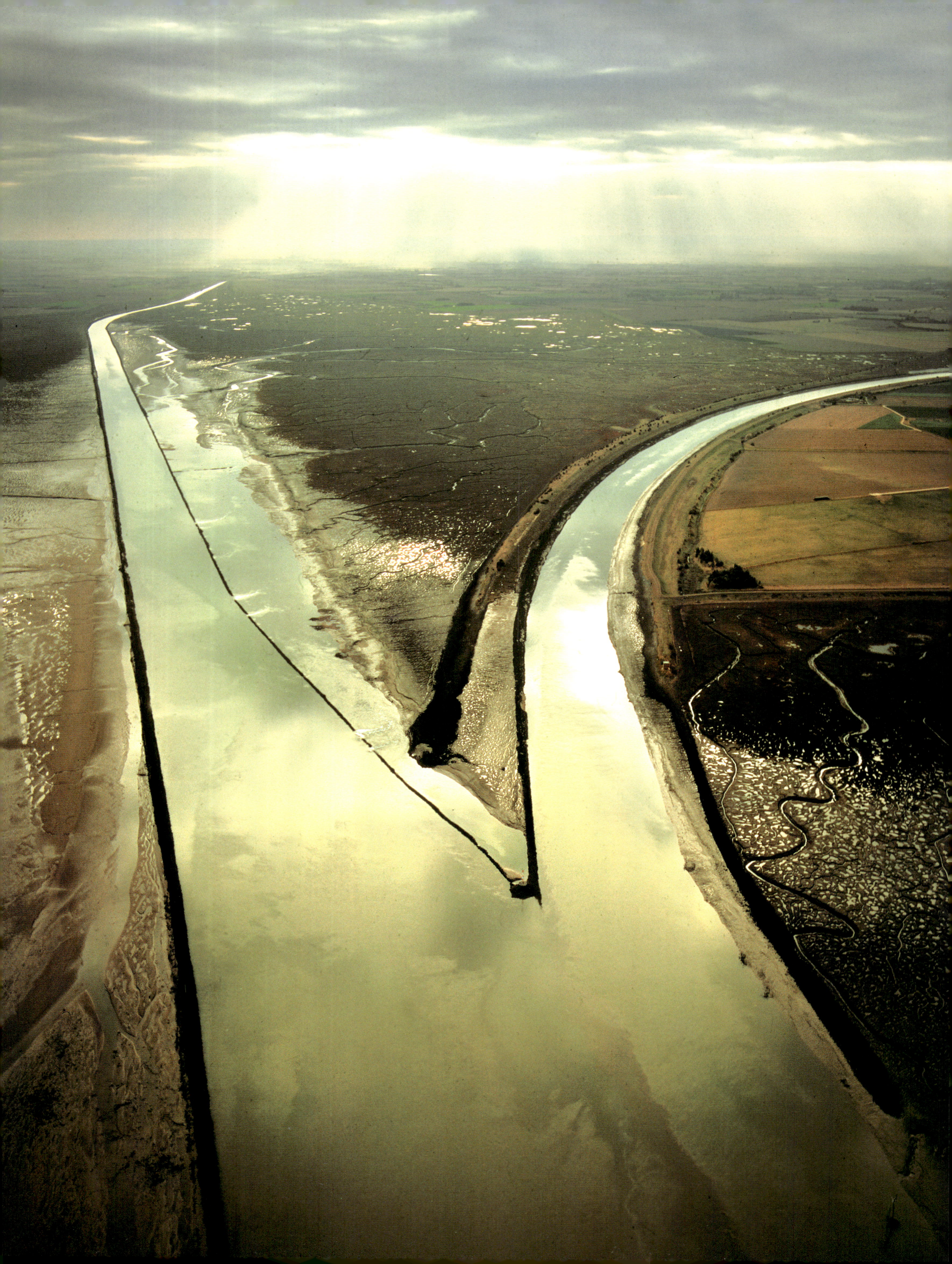

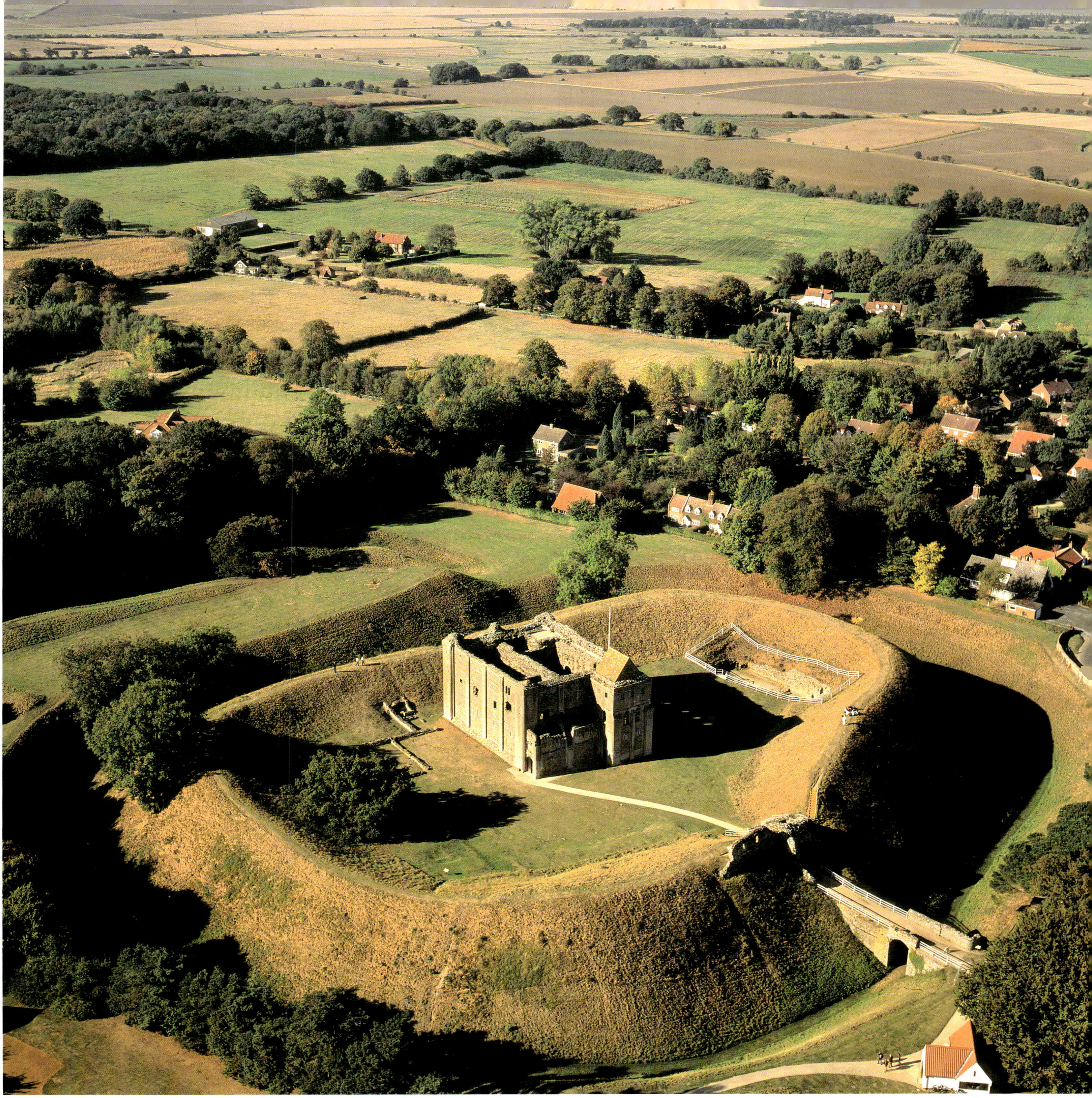

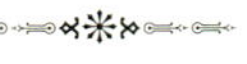

THE WASH (LEFT)

SINCE ROMAN TIMES, efforts have been made to control flooding and indeed reclaim land from the sea by creating dykes and channels to drain the marshes of the Fens. Rich, dark land criss-crossed by a network of water channels draining into The Wash stretches across wide open spaces beneath a huge sky. The Wash is a large shallow bay with mudflats, saltmarsh and tidal inlets, a haven for birds. The photograph shows the south-western corner where tidal channels drain on to Black Buoy sand.

CASTLE RISING (ABOVE)

THE MAGNIFICENT KEEP AT CASTLE RISING was built in 1140 by William d'Albigny. The castle itself, with its impressive earthbanks and ditches, was to become one of the most important in East Anglia, boasting a long list of distinguished and royal guests with Isabella, Queen of Edward II, its most famous resident. By 1572, a survey reported to Queen Elizabeth I that it was decaying and increasingly in ruin. It was only in the 20th century, however, that any extensive work was undertaken to arrest further decay of this special place.

WELLS-NEXT-THE-SEA (OVERLEAF)

A NORFOLK VILLAGE, SMALL PORT AND A SEASIDE RESORT situated by a long wide channel about 1.5km (1 mile) from the sea. The name Wells comes from the fresh water springs that rise in the town. Trapped in the underlying chalk the springs provided a supply of fresh water for the town, and many houses had their own well. The village is picturesque with a mix of old and new brightly coloured beach huts and the quay with its local boats. The area has been designated an Area of Outstanding Natural Beauty.

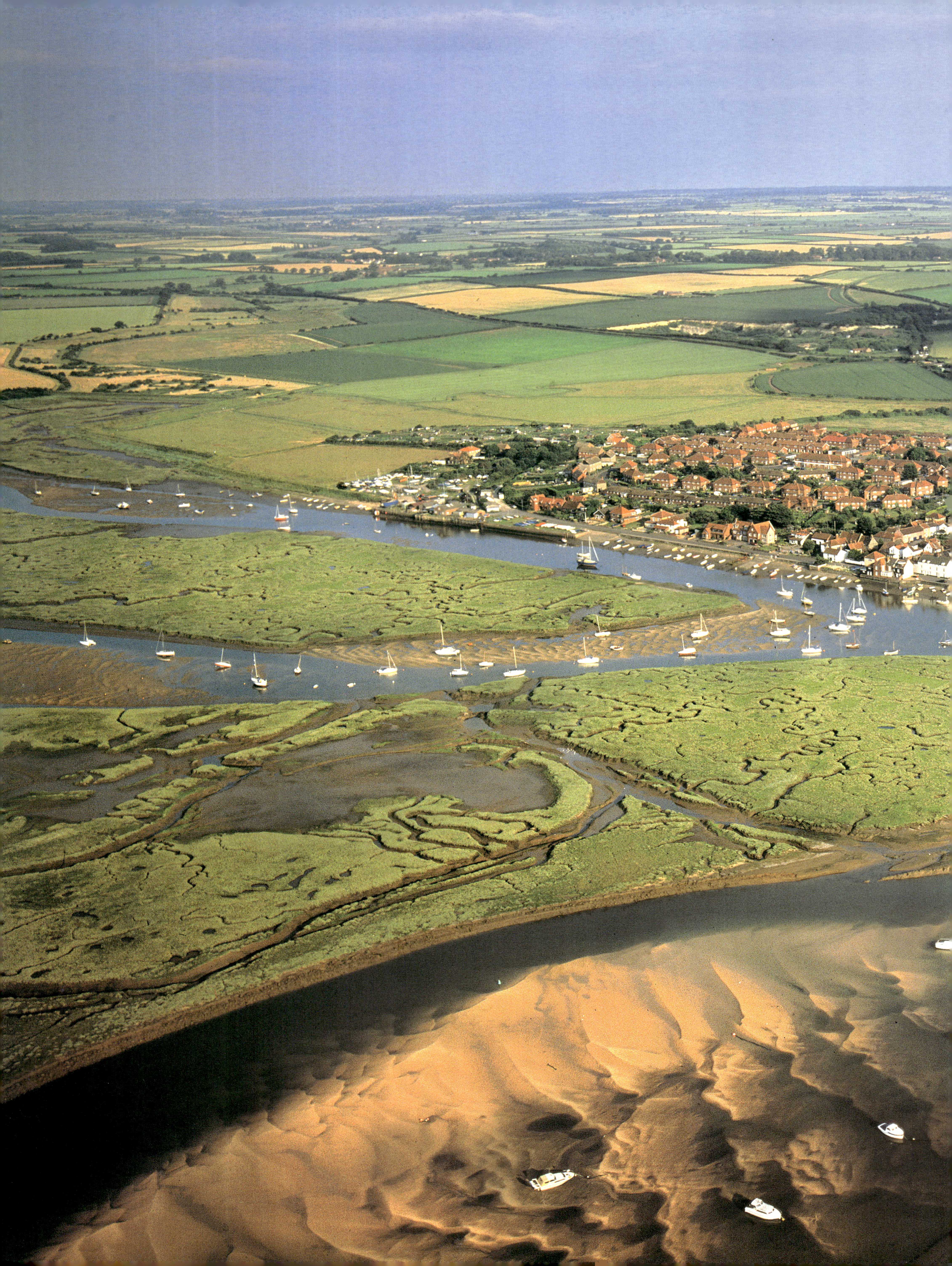

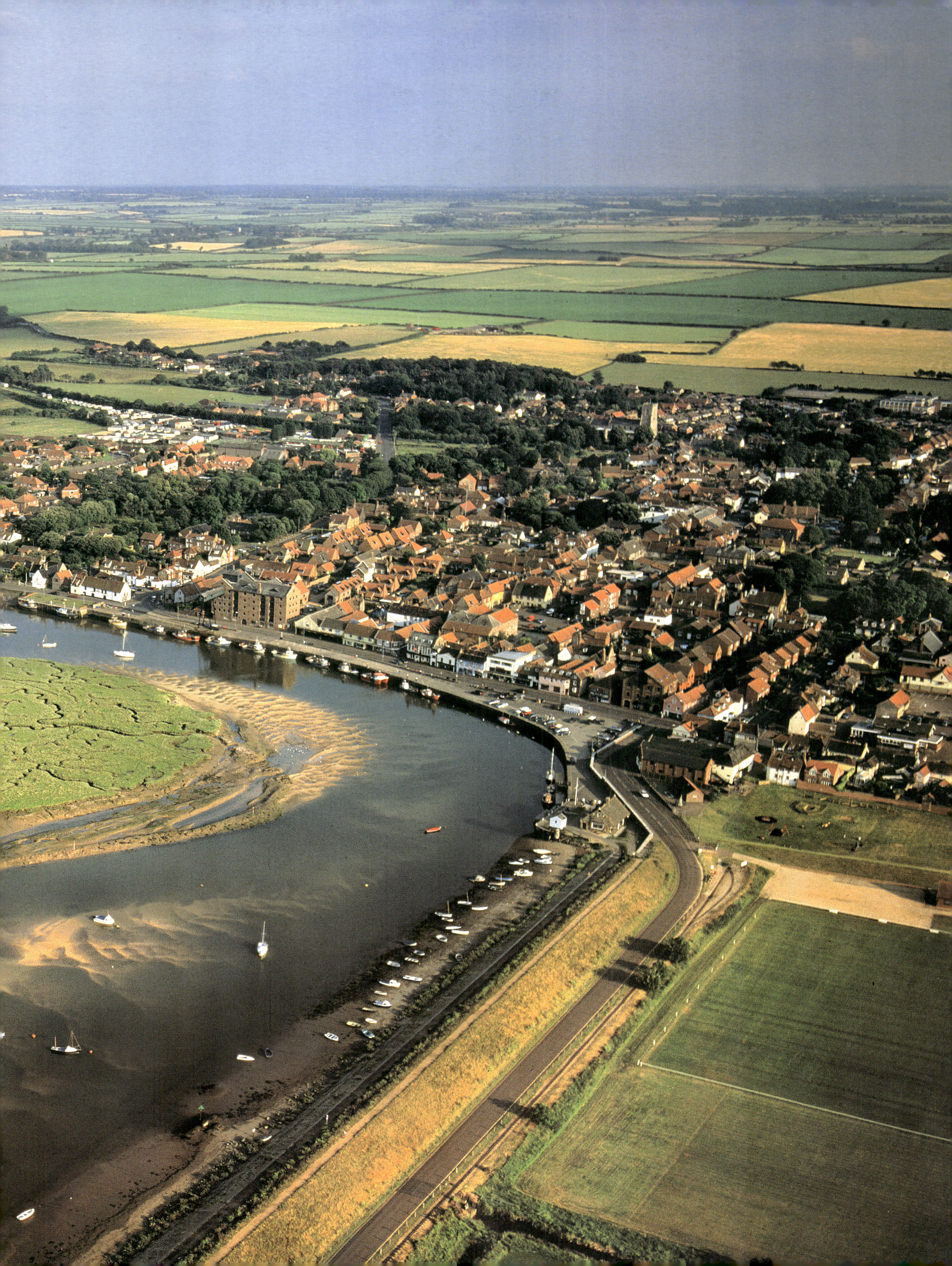

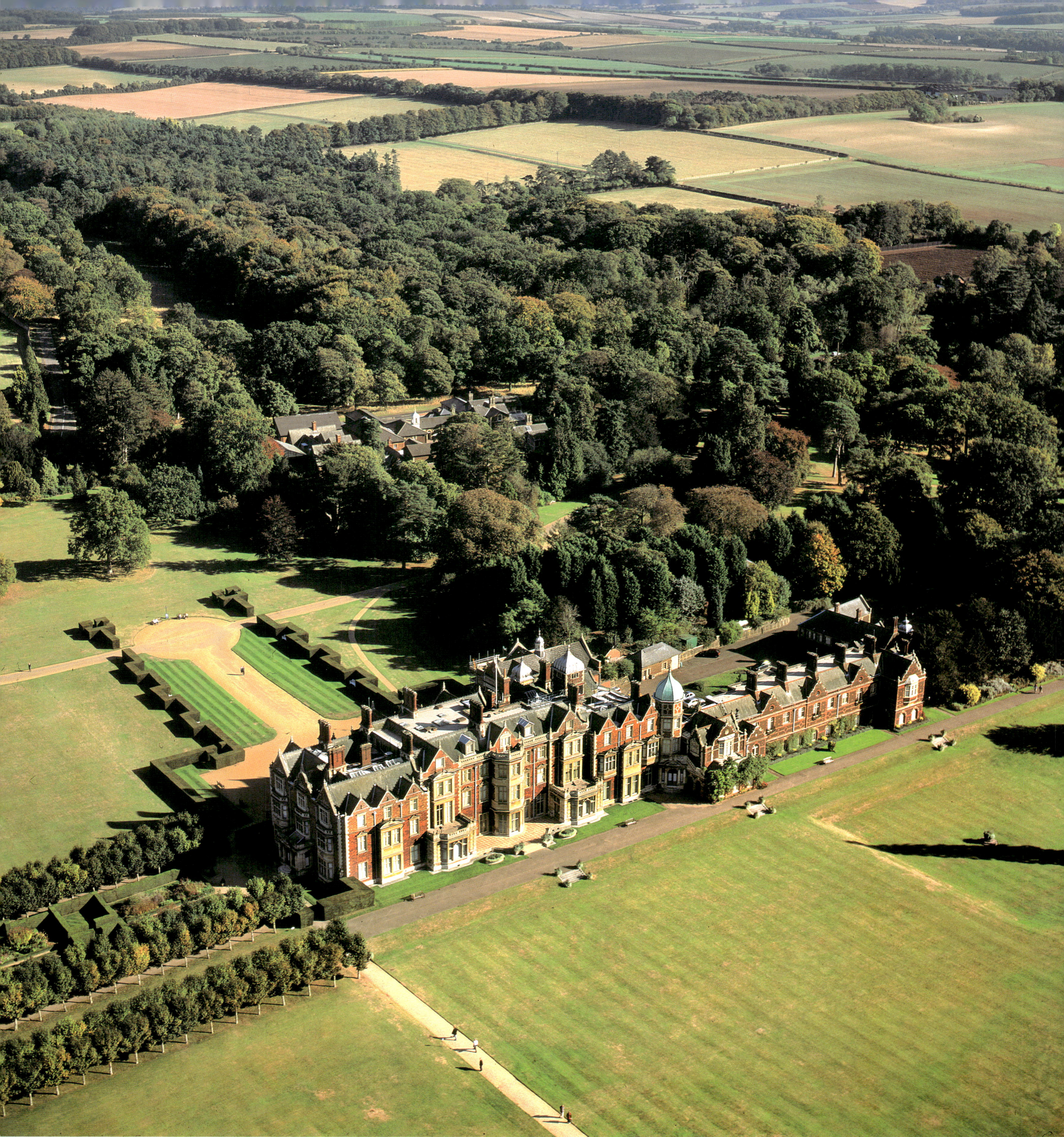

SANDRINGHAM HOUSE (ABOVE)

SANDRINGHAM HOUSE IN NORFOLK, originally a Georgian structure, has been the private home of four generations of sovereigns since 1862. The Queen and other members of the royal family regularly spend Christmas at Sandringham and make it their official base until February each year. It was at Sandringham that the Queen's father, King George VI, died on February 6 1952. When the royal family is not in residence, the house is open to the public.

HOLKHAM HALL (RIGHT)

HOLKHAM HALL, A LARGE STATELY HOME occupied by seven generations of the Earls of Leicester, is a large Palladian palace built in the mid 1700s. The grounds are extensive (over 3,000 acres) and were landscaped by Capability Brown who created the lake and planted thousands of trees. Here, large herds of fallow deer roam and there are many species of wildfowl on the lake. Part of the estate is a National Nature Reserve incorporating extensive salt marshes.

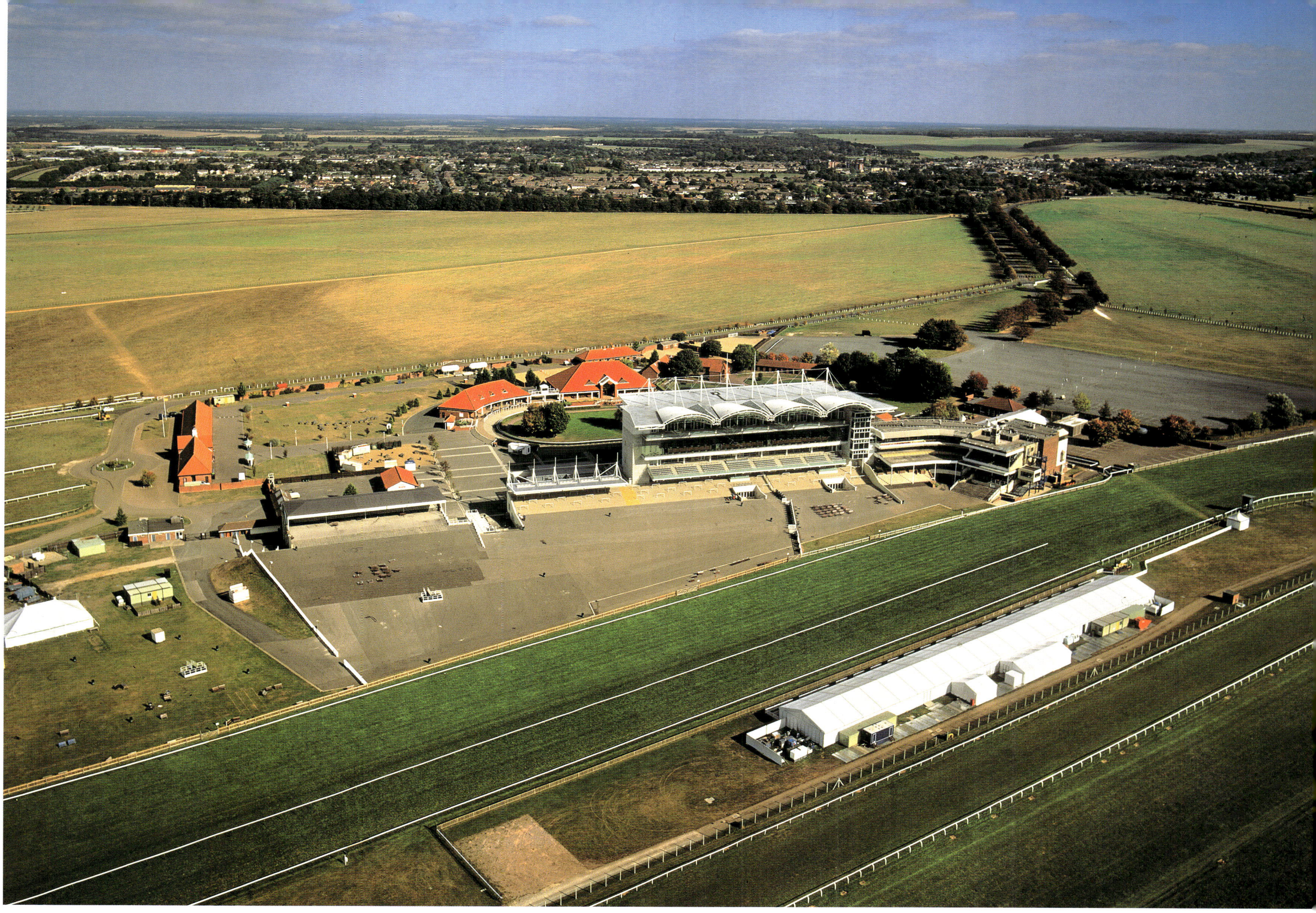

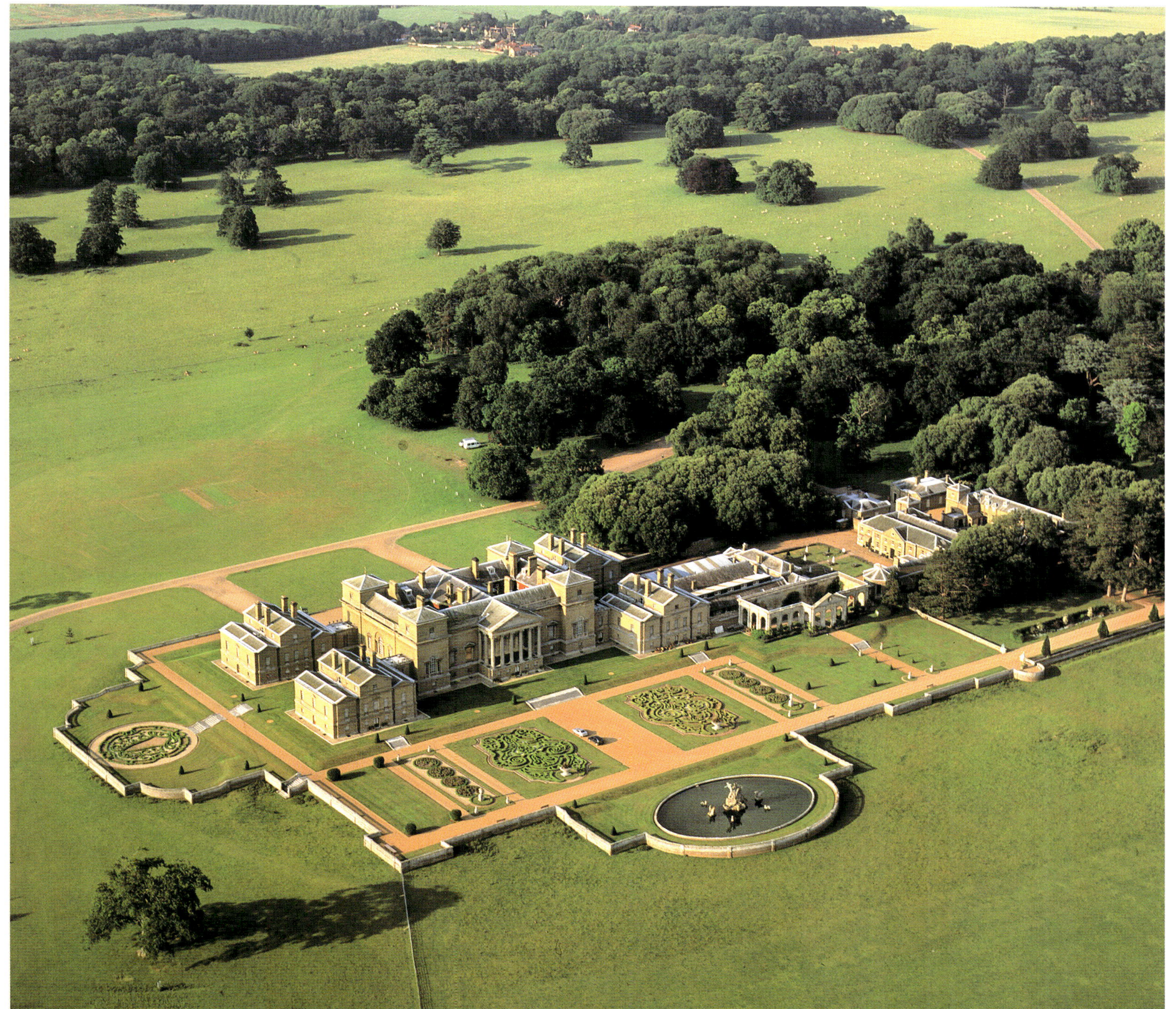

NEWMARKET RACECOURSE (ABOVE)

NEWMARKET RACECOURSE has been the scene of many great horse races for over three centuries. The historic racecourse, the Rowley Mile, is named after King Charles II ("Old Rowley") who founded the Newmarket meetings following his restoration to the throne in 1660. Everything connected with racing is here: it is home to the National Stud, the British Racing School, the original headquarters of the Jockey Club, and up to 3,000 horses are constantly in training in the area.

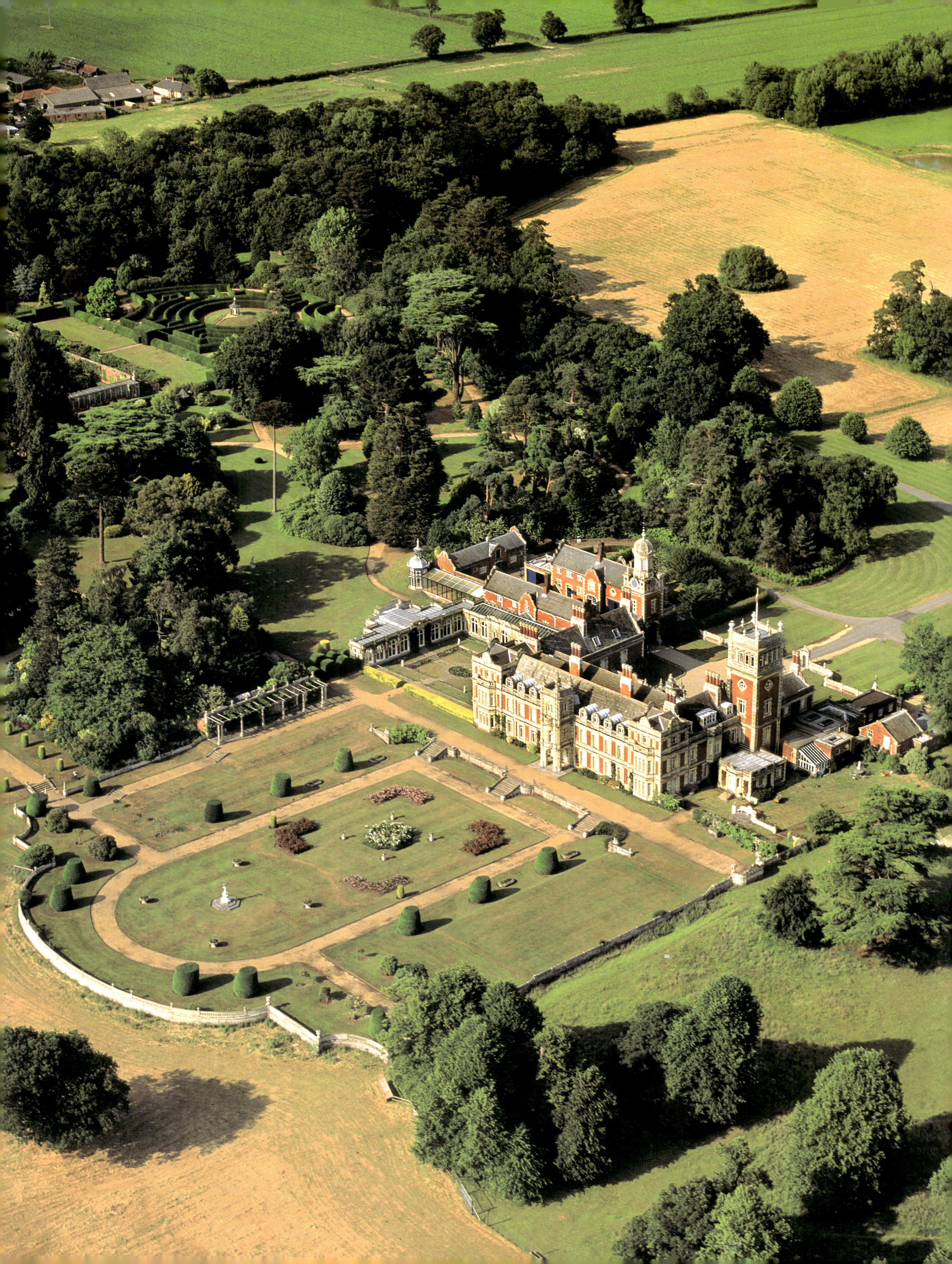

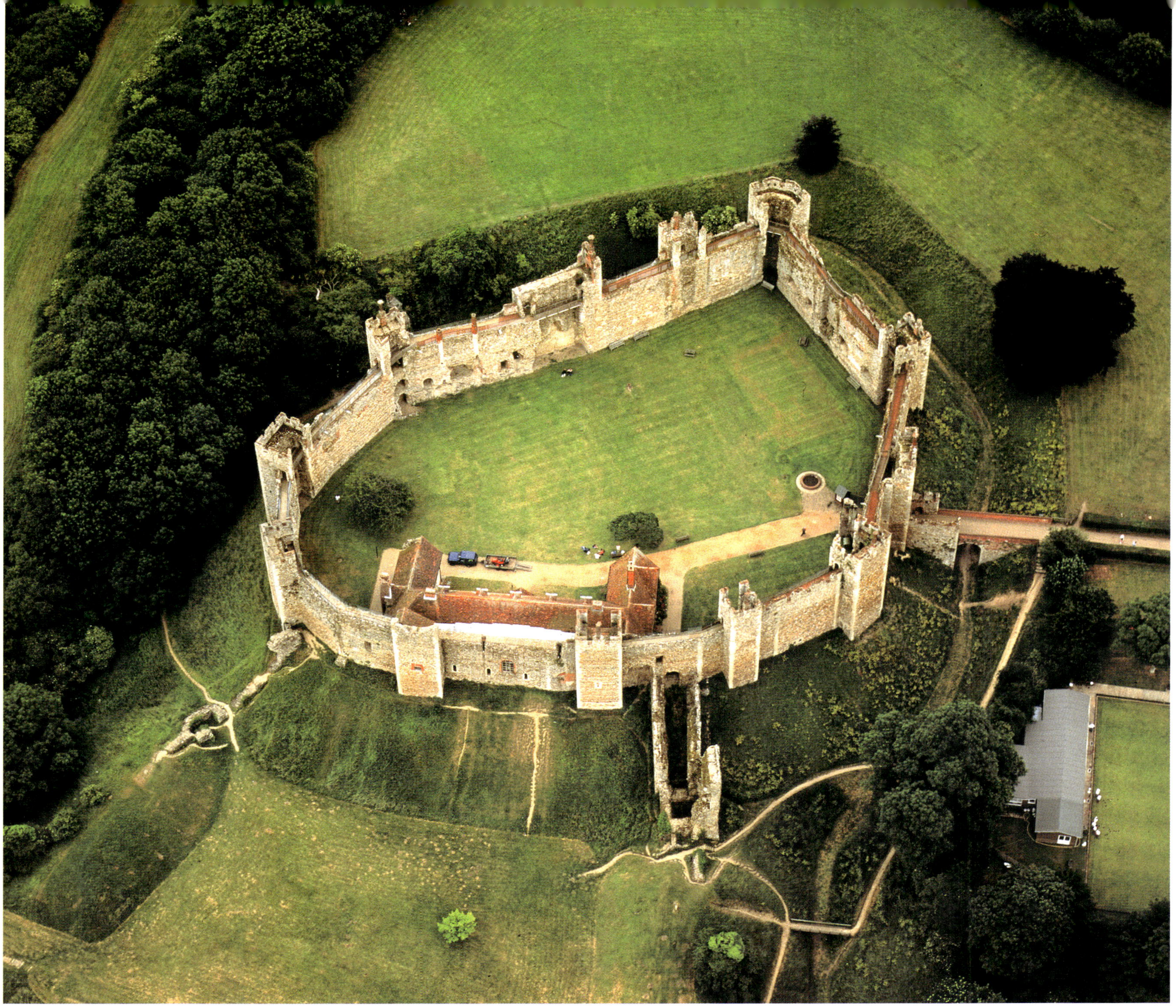

FRAMLINGHAM CASTLE (LEFT)

ROGER BIGOD BUILT THE CASTLE, between 1189 and 1200, to replace his father's castle which was destroyed by order of Henry II in 1175. The castle has a very impressive series of 12 towers (a 13th collapsed) set along the length of a magnificent curtain wall that looks today much as it would have done 800 years ago. In the lower bailey stands the Prison Tower and a gatehouse with a spiral stairwell, both projecting from the curtain wall. A wide, deep ditch and a very large outer bailey encase the rest of the curtain wall. Mary Tudor - "Bloody Mary" - was proclaimed Queen of England here in July 1553.

SOMERLEYTON HALL (LEFT)

SOMERLEYTON HALL IN SUFFOLK stands on the site of an earlier Jacobean manor house but it was transformed by Sir Morton Peto between 1844 and 1851 and now is unmistakably early Victorian. For the work on Somerleyton, Sir Morton employed John Thomas, a sculptor and ornamental mason who worked on the Houses of Parliament. The gardens have long been considered excellent, and one of the most popular features is the yew hedge maze, one of the finest in Britain (see picture on page 1).

MELFORD HALL (RIGHT)

IN THE MIDDLE AGES THE MANOR OF MELFORD in Suffolk belonged to the Benedictine abbey of Bury St Edmunds. After the dissolution of the monasteries by Henry VIII it was granted to Sir William Cordell. He extended the house in 1554 and when completed he entertained Queen Elizabeth I here. Despite the removal of the gatehouse and the disappearance of part of the moat, the exterior of Melford Hall is very much as it was when Elizabeth visited.

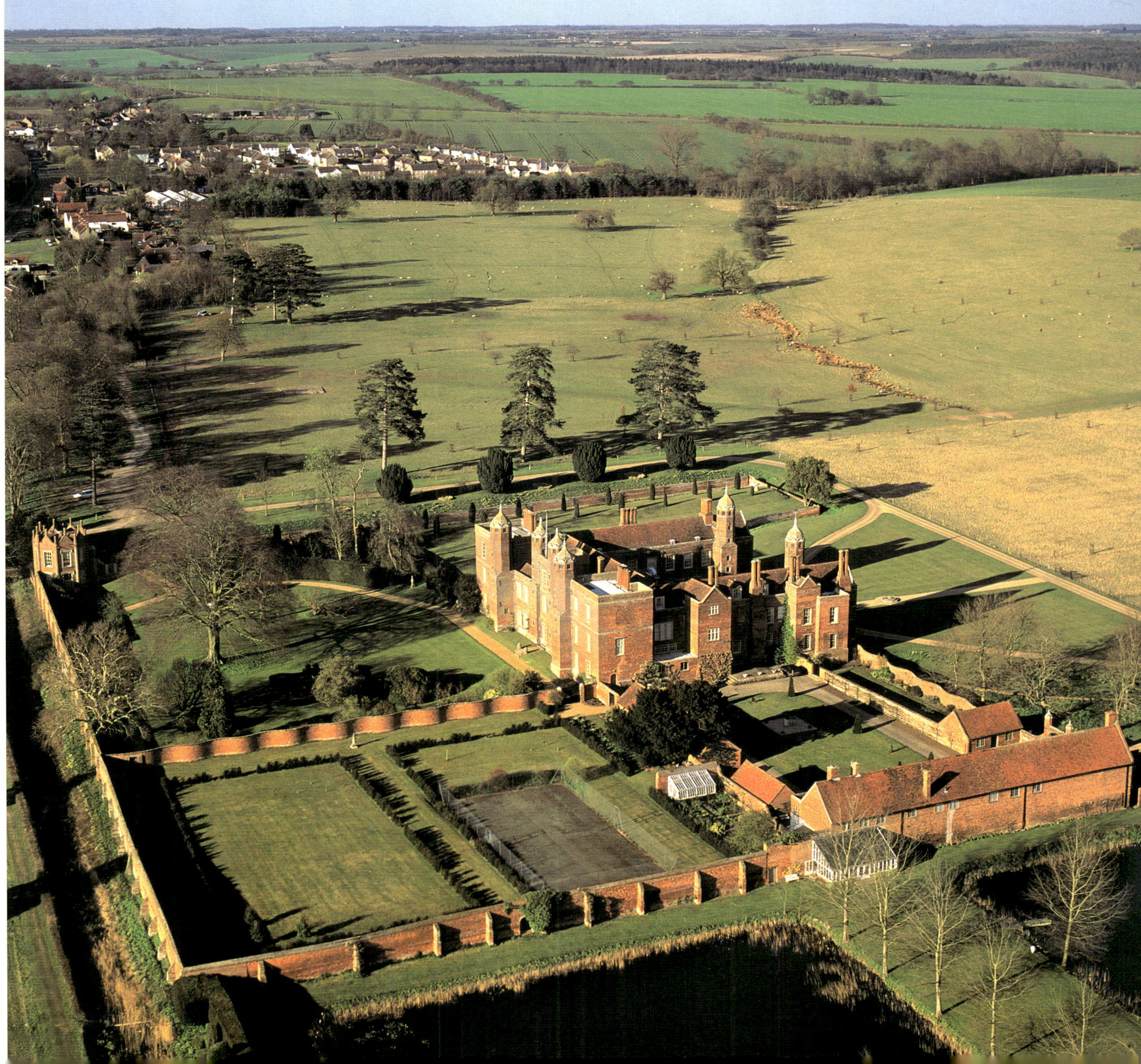

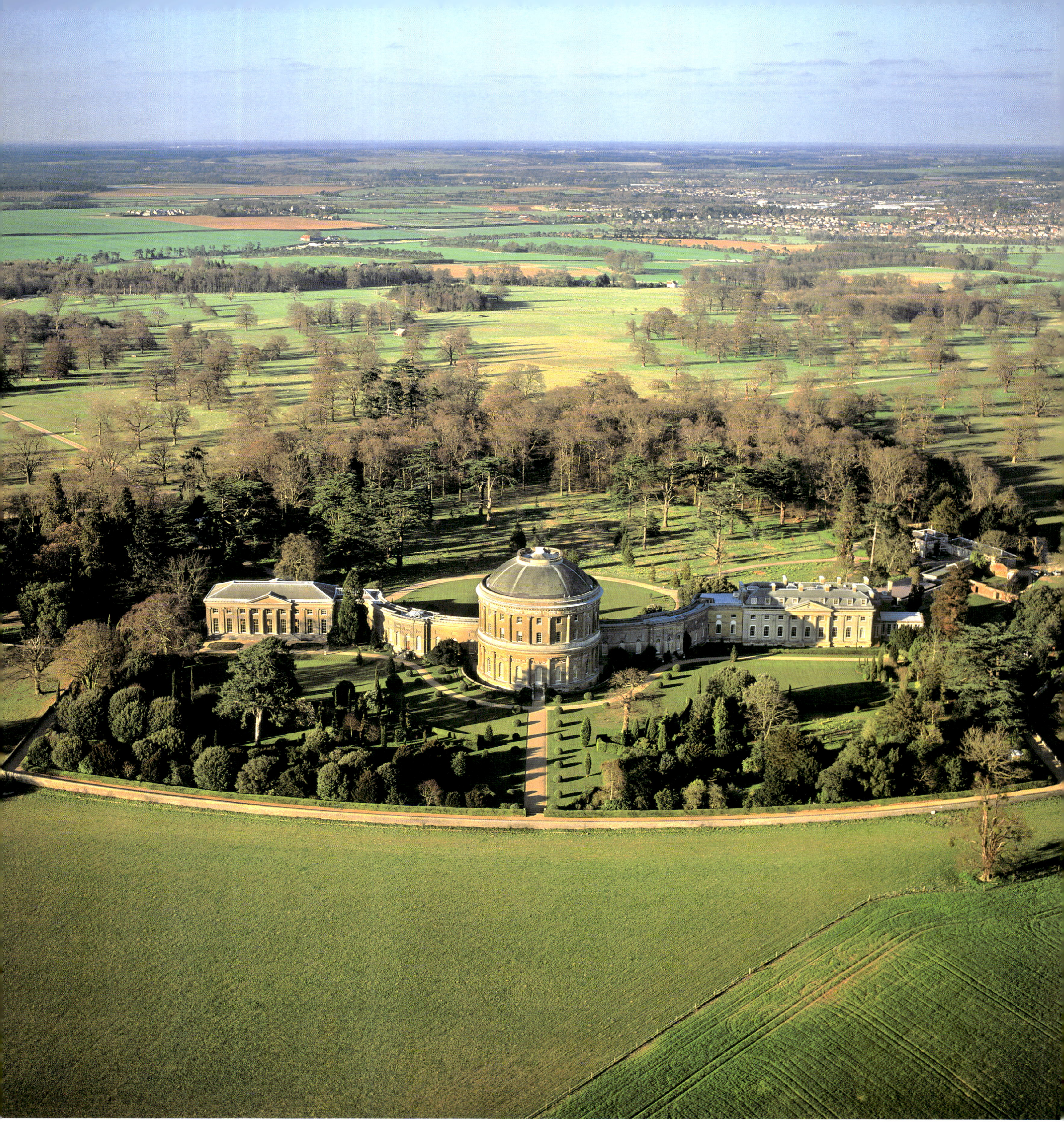

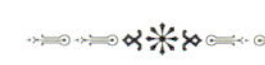

ICKWORTH (ABOVE)

ICKWORTH HOUSE IN SUFFOLK is a spectacular Italian-style house set within English parkland. The estate, comprising 1,800 acres, was owned by the Hervey family from the 15th to the 20th century. The present house was built in 1795 by the famously eccentric Frederick Hervey, 4th Earl of Bristol and Bishop of Derry. The extraordinary central rotunda and curving wings were intended to house treasures collected from all over Europe.

COLCHESTER CASTLE (RIGHT)

CONSTRUCTED OVER THE MASSIVE VAULTS of the ruined Temple of Claudius, Colchester Castle has the largest Norman keep in Europe. Measuring some 46m by 34m and built largely from stone and brick quarried from the old Roman town of Colchester, the castle is believed to be the work of Gundulph, Bishop of Rochester, around 1076. He was also responsible for the design of the White Tower at the Tower of London.

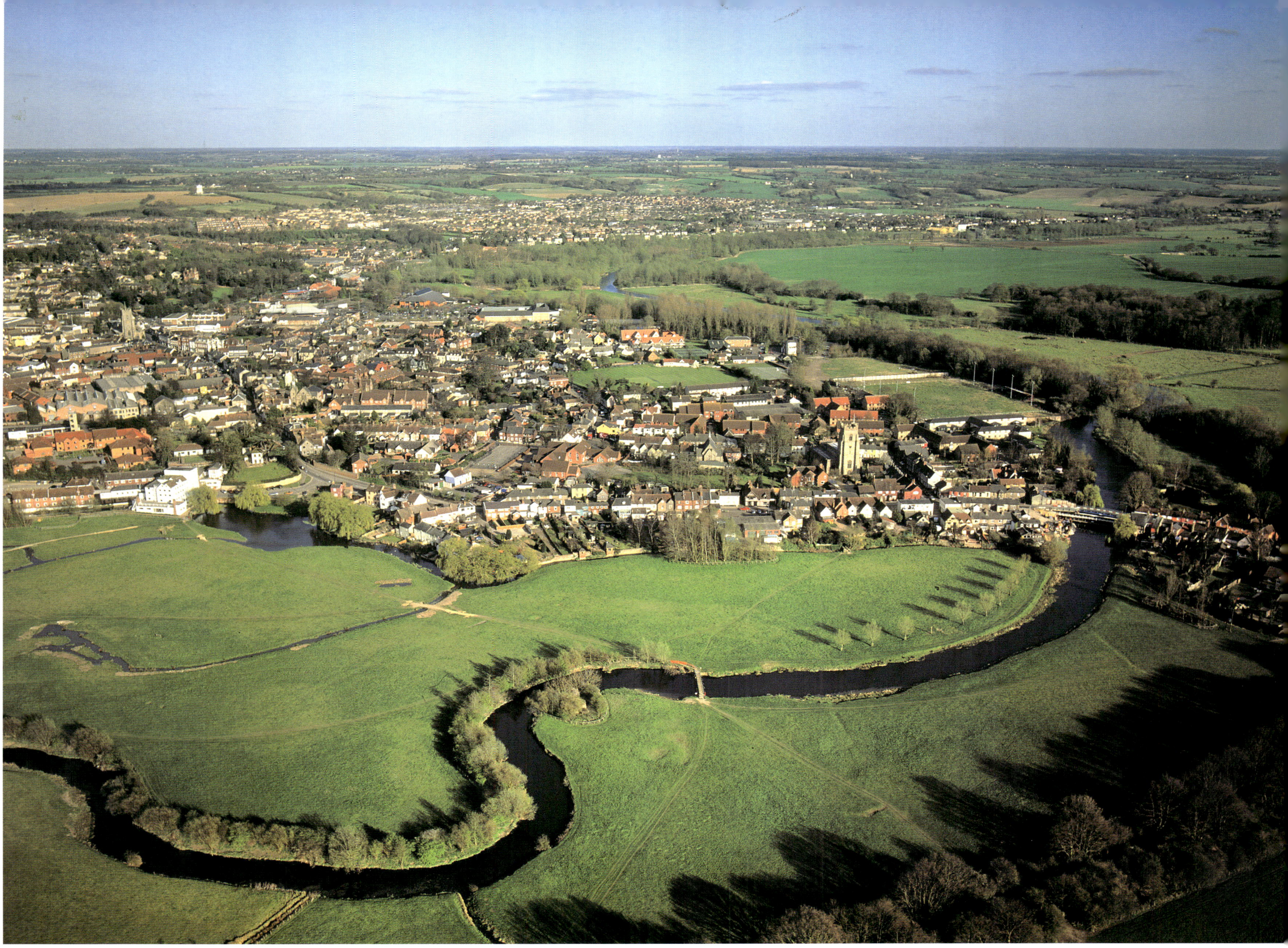

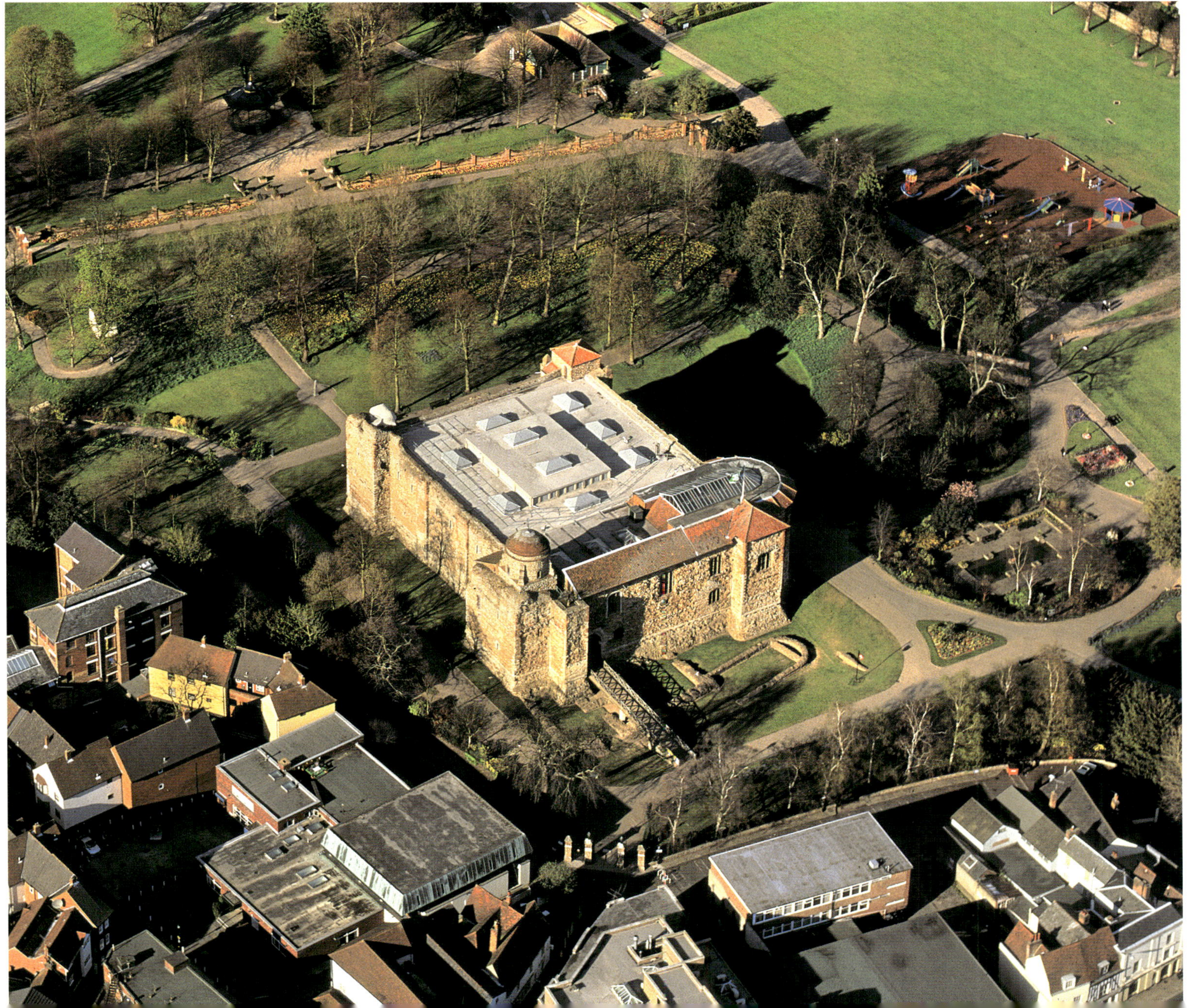

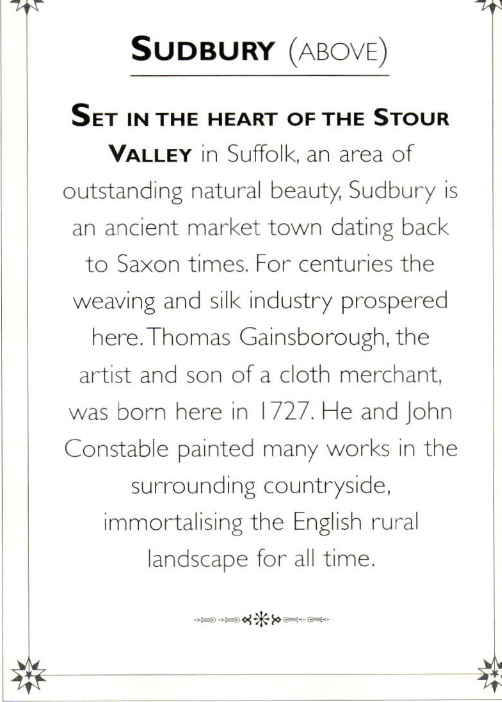

SUDBURY (ABOVE)

SET IN THE HEART OF THE STOUR VALLEY in Suffolk, an area of outstanding natural beauty, Sudbury is an ancient market town dating back to Saxon times. For centuries the weaving and silk industry prospered here. Thomas Gainsborough, the artist and son of a cloth merchant, was born here in 1727. He and John Constable painted many works in the surrounding countryside, immortalising the English rural landscape for all time.

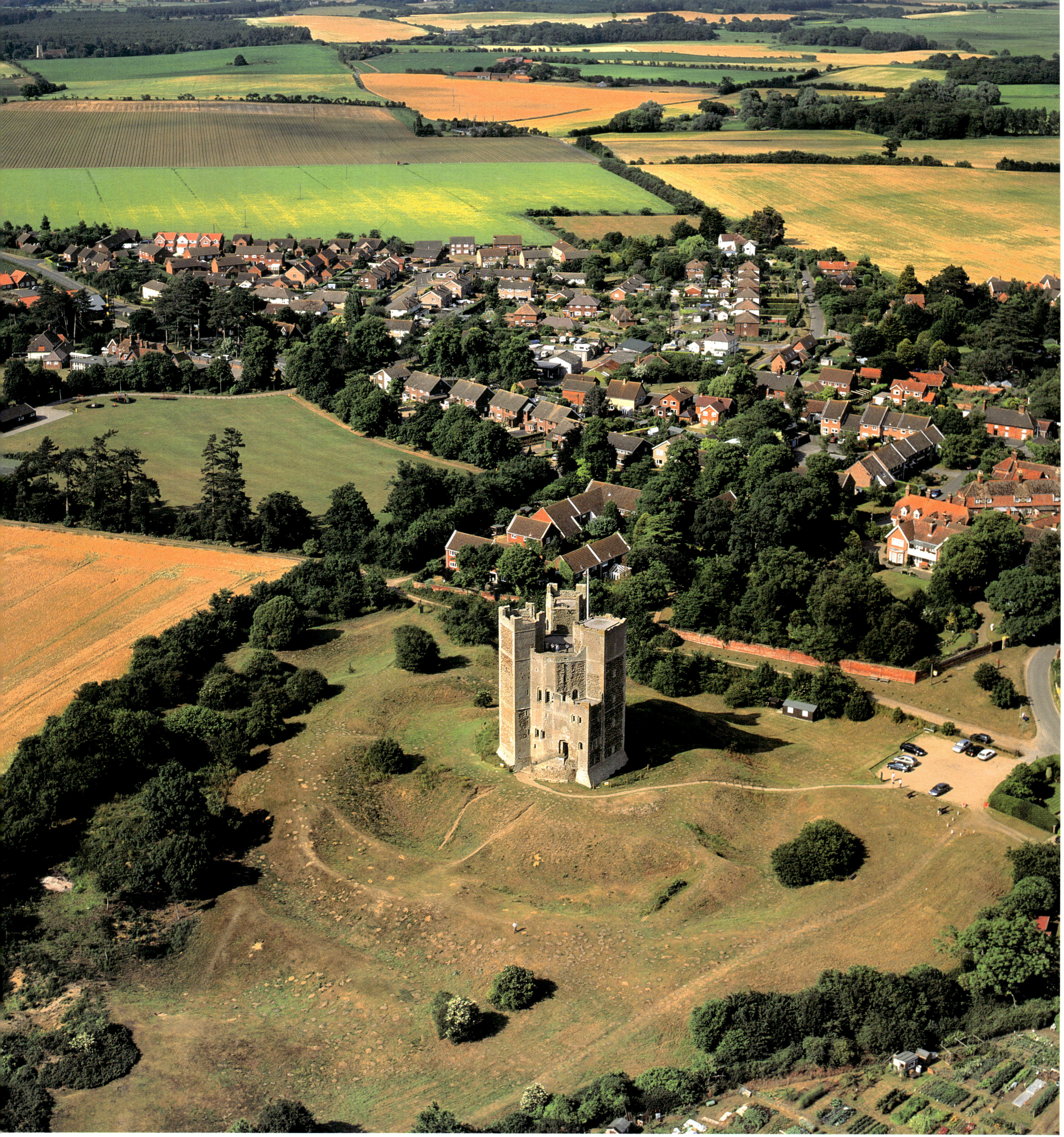

ORFORD CASTLE (ABOVE)

AT THE TIME OF THE DOMESDAY BOOK, the small Suffolk town of Orford was just a tiny hamlet. One hundred years later, under the influence of Henry II, it became a busy port. Work began on the castle in 1165 and the marshes were also drained. The keep at Orford has many individual features such as the complex rectangular turrets and it was the most expensive of Henry's castles. In 1962 it passed into state guardianship and is now maintained by English Heritage.

ORFORD BEACH (RIGHT)

ORFORD BEACH IS THE LONGEST VEGETATED SHINGLE SPIT in Europe, home of a significant number of rare plant communities and an important breeding site for migrant birds. The Suffolk coast is one of the most fragile regions in Britain, some parts being eroded while others are silting up. Under the influence of the North Sea, Orford Beach moves steadily southward. The delicate heathland is protected by law, but its eco-system is threatened by thoughtless visitors.

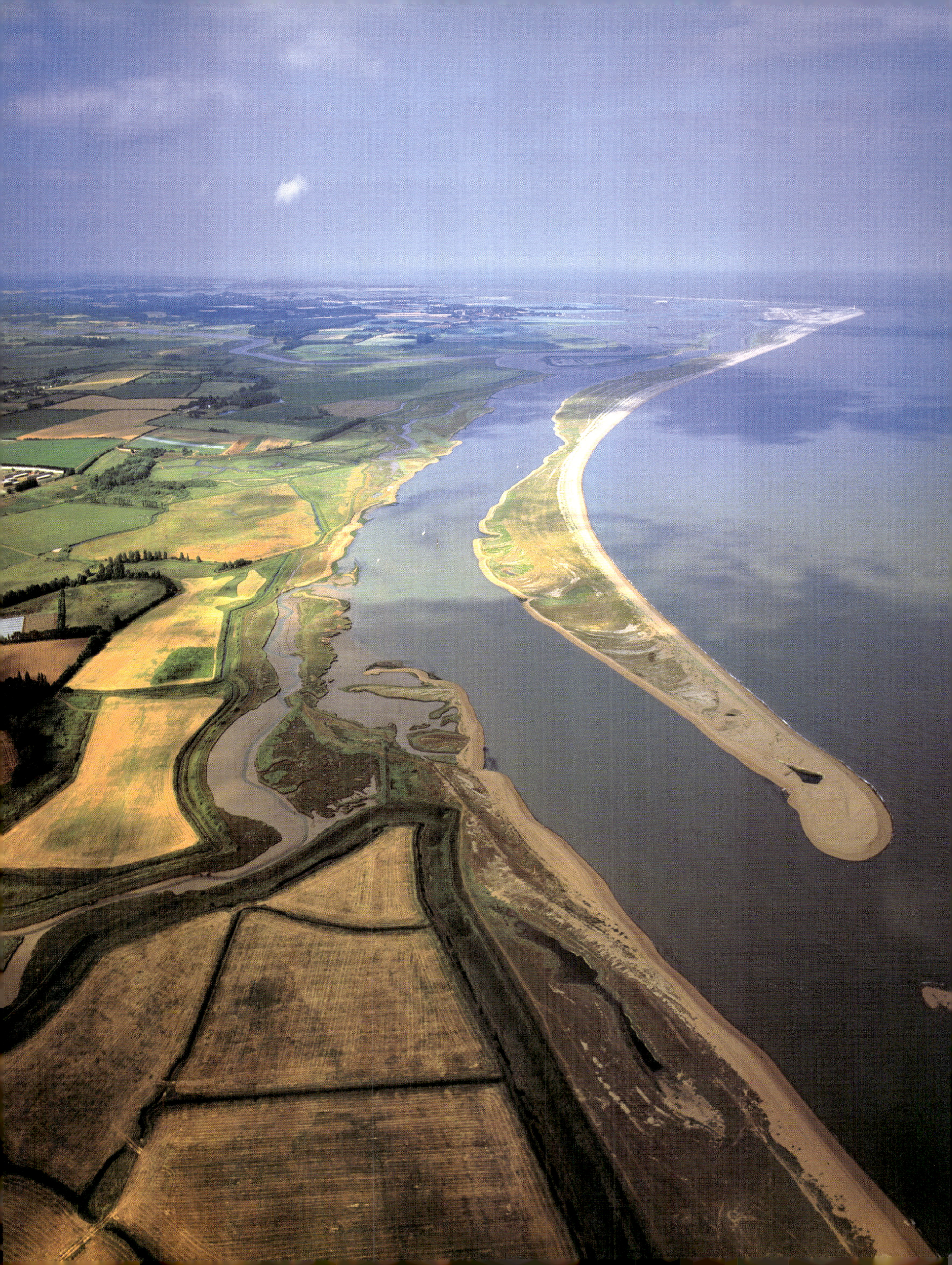

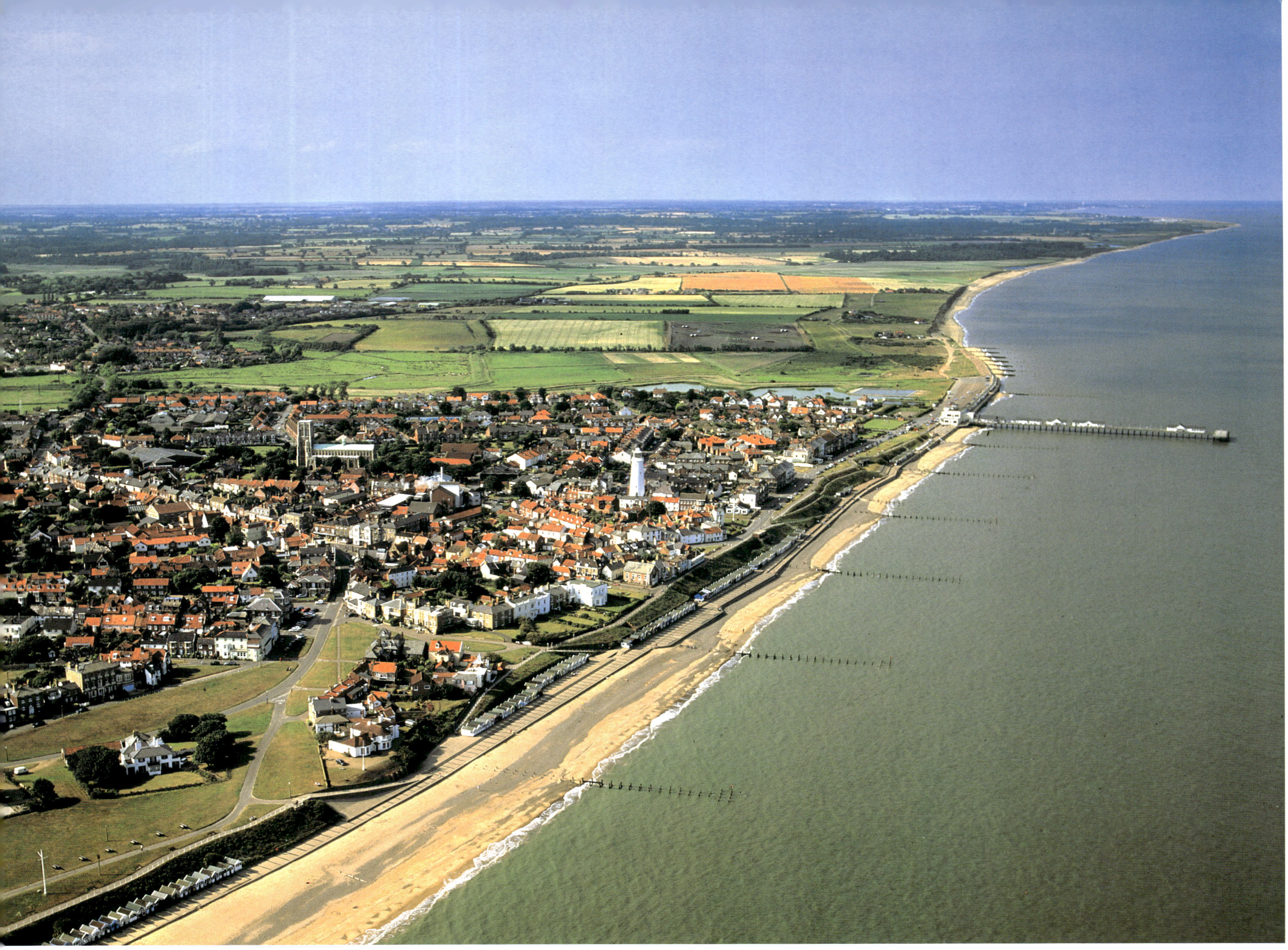

SOUTHWOLD (ABOVE)

SOUTHWOLD, AN ANCIENT
TOWN that is now a seaside
resort, has one of the country's
most famous piers, built in
1900. It also has a magnificent
whitewashed lighthouse which
commenced operation in 1890
and was illuminated by paraffin
until 1938. A prosperous
fishing port in the 11th
Century, fishing boats still
operate from the harbour, with
fresh fish regularly on sale along
the Blackshore area.

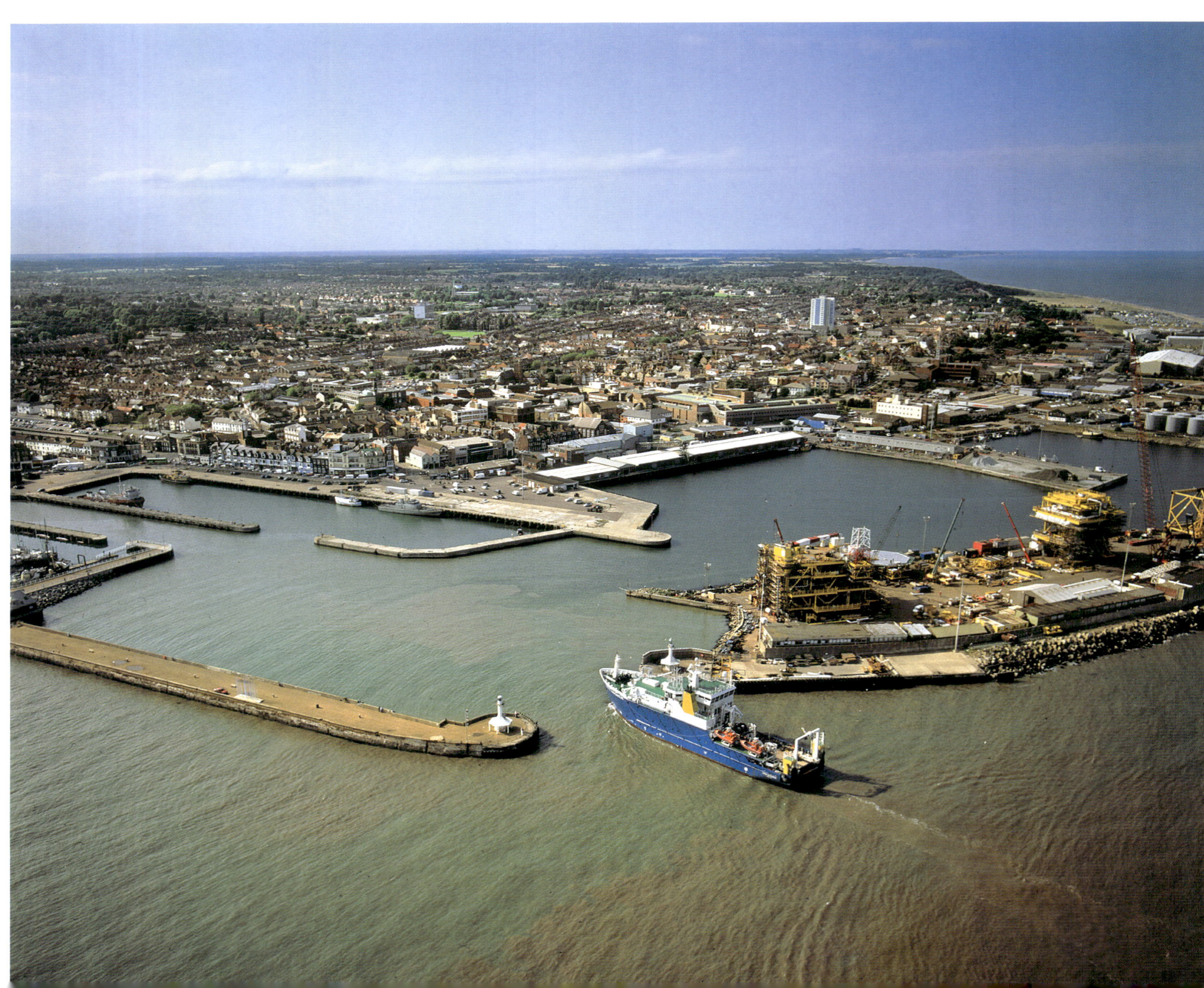

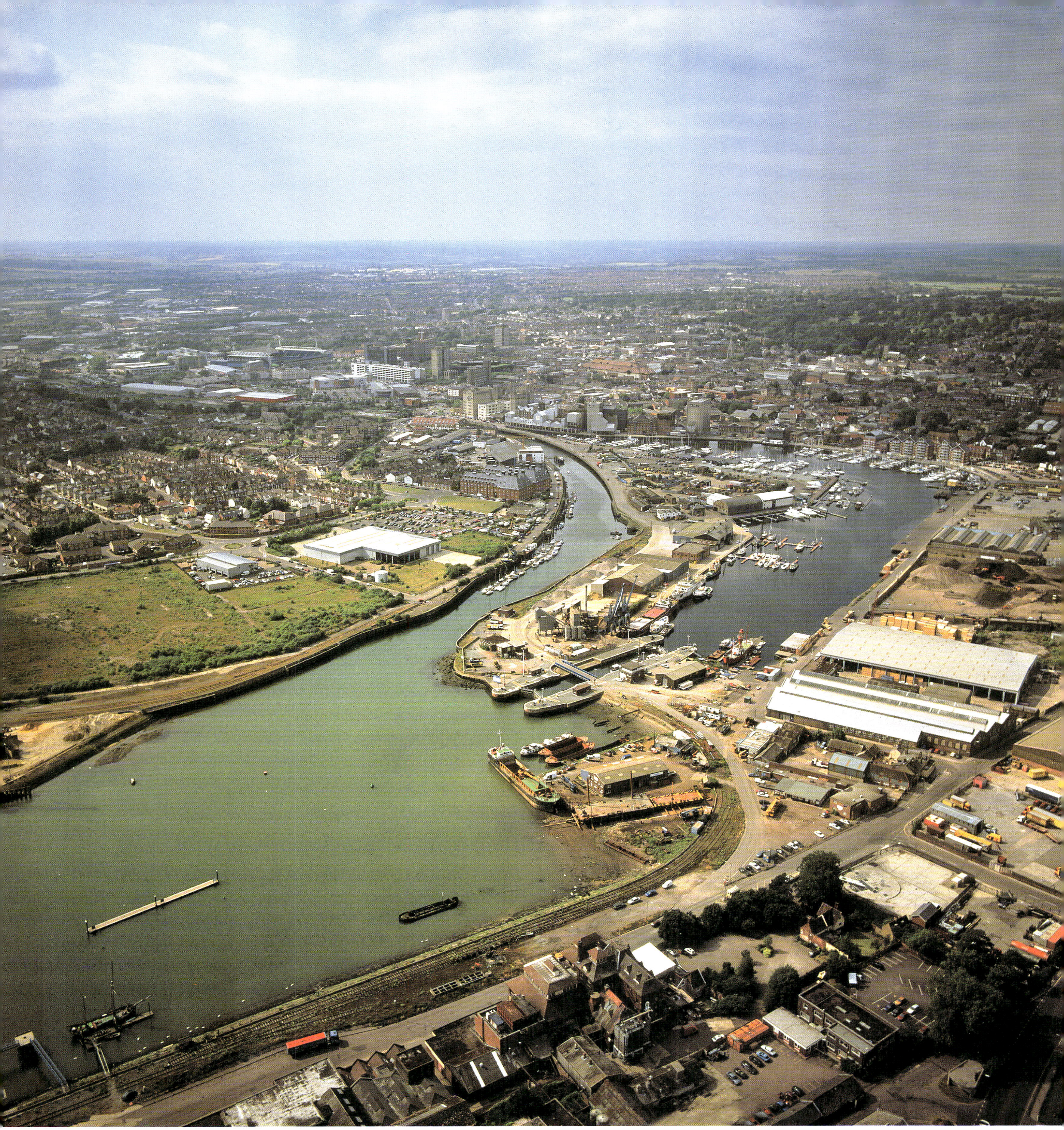

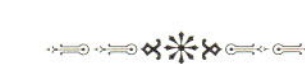

LOWESTOFT (LEFT)

LOWESTOFT, IN SUFFOLK, IS THE FURTHEST EAST you can travel in England. It was a fishing port until the herring fishing industry collapsed, but now supports North Sea oil rigs. During both world wars, the town was bombed heavily. Offshore, several German U-boats were sunk and many fishermen helped in the evacuation from Dunkirk. The area has been notorious for shipwrecks and the North Light was the site of the first lighthouse in England.

IPSWICH (ABOVE)

IPSWICH IS THE COUNTY TOWN OF SUFFOLK, yet it has no cathedral and no castle. However, it was a borough before the Norman conquest and a charter was granted by King John in 1200. Today it is a major port and one of the fastest growing market towns in Suffolk. Although the centre has been redeveloped, some of the original town has been preserved and a cluster of old narrow streets with timber clad houses still remain.

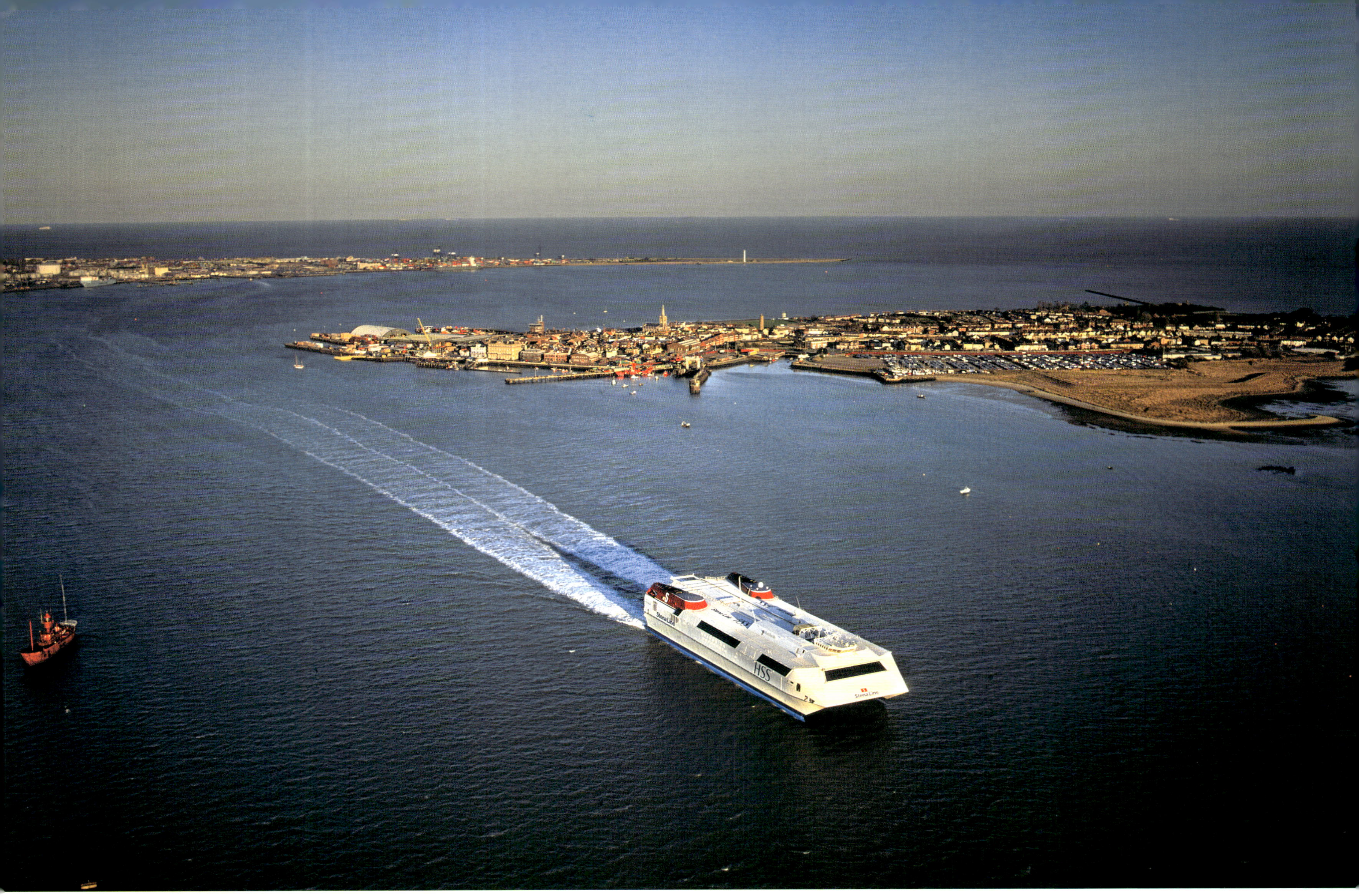

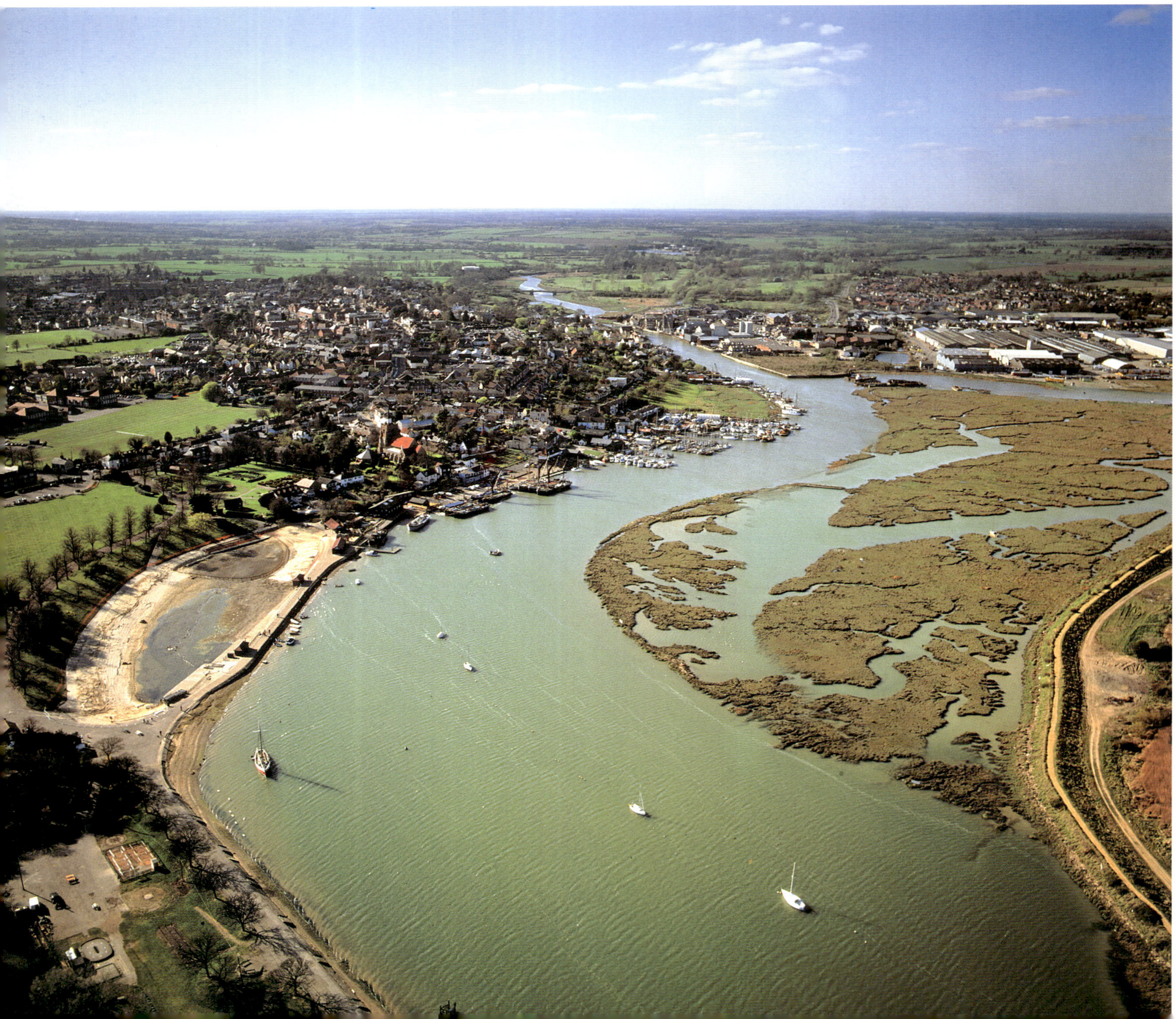

HARWICH HARBOUR
(ABOVE)

HARWICH, IN ESSEX, is situated where the river Stour and the river Orwell join to enter the North Sea. The town is protected by a peninsula which stretches south from Felixstowe. Many distinguished seafarers have set out from here: Newport sailed with Raleigh and Jones was the Master on the Mayflower. Harwich was already a town in medieval times and is now a port for ferries to the Continent.

MALDON (LEFT)

MALDON, IN ESSEX, stands on a hill on the south bank of the River Blackwater which becomes a wide estuary before entering the North Sea. This was the site of the battle of Maldon in 991 when the Anglo-Saxons were defeated by the Danes. Maldon's name has Saxon origins, *dun* being the word for hill. Today it is a picturesque town and fishing port where historic Thames sailing barges may frequently be seen.

WEST MERSEA (RIGHT)

MERSEA ISLAND, WHICH INCLUDES the town of West Mersea and the village of East Mersea, is known for its oyster fishing industry. It is located in the estuary of the rivers Blackwater and Colne, approximately 14km (9 miles) south-east of Colchester. The island can be reached by an artificial causeway known as the Strood, which was built in 700; it is the only link with the mainland which is liable to flooding at high tide. The name Mersea is a derivation of the word *meresig* which dates from the early 10th century and means "island of the pool".

CLACTON-ON-SEA (BELOW)

CLACTON-ON-SEA IS A TYPICAL ESSEX seaside town, with a large pier built in 1871. It buzzes with holidaymakers in summer, drawn by miles of sandy beaches. As a resort it developed in the late 19th century: by 1882 the town had a railway branch line, crucial to the development of the resort. The town saw its heyday between the two world wars. Then in the 1960s, Mods and Rockers staged running-battles among day-trippers which brought unwelcome headlines.

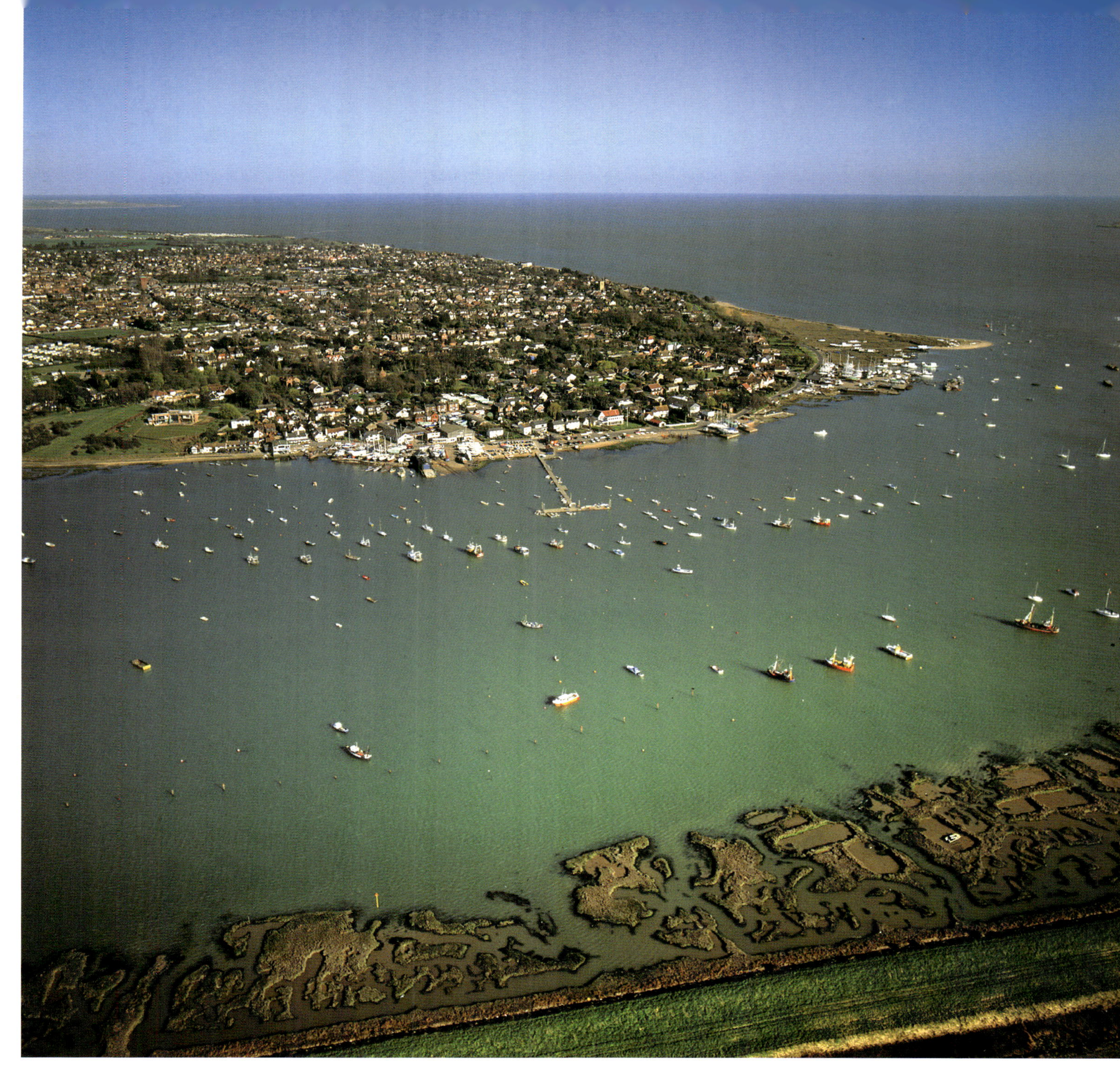

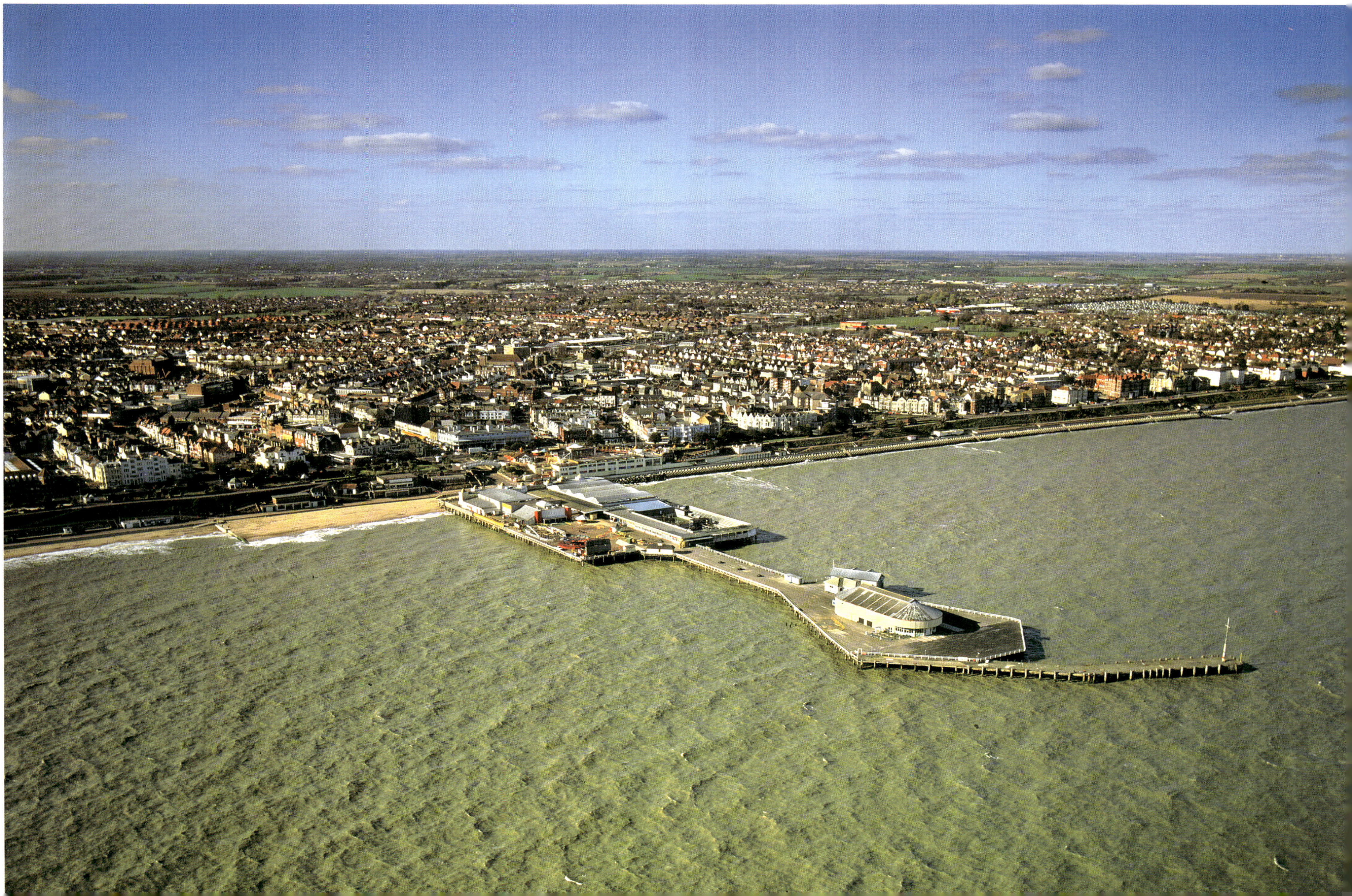

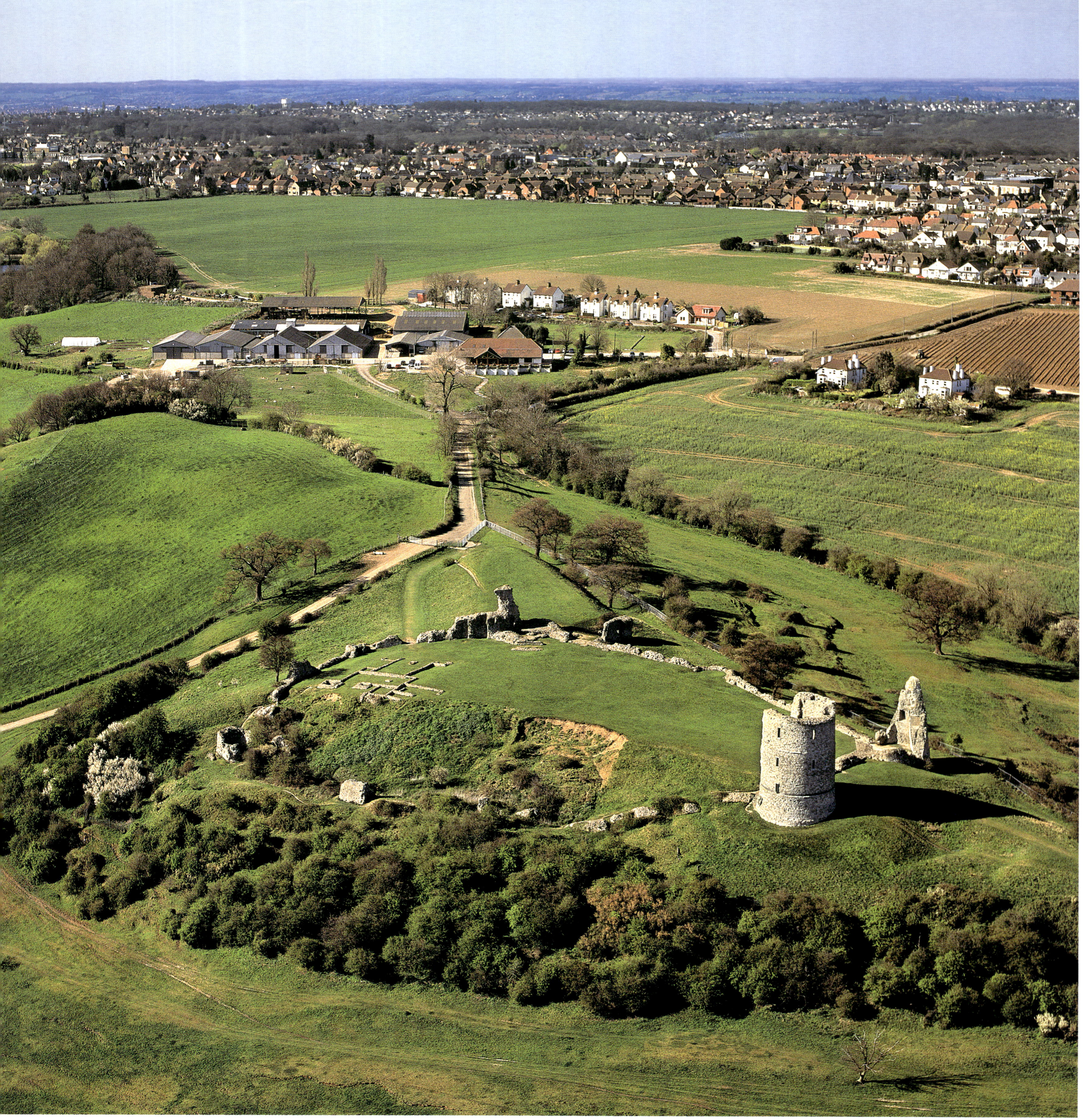

Hadleigh Castle (ABOVE)

THE RUINS OF TWO TOWERS, one standing almost to its original height, and some of the curtain wall are all that remain of Hadleigh Castle overlooking the Thames estuary. It was built in 1230 for Hubert de Burgh, who had been Chief Justiciar to King John and acted as regent for the young King Henry III. Later it became royal property and by tradition the tenants of Hadleigh were the king's consorts, most notably belonging to three of King Henry VIII's wives: Catherine of Aragon, Anne of Cleves and Catherine Parr.

Southend-on-Sea (RIGHT)

SOUTHEND WAS ONCE THE MOST POPULAR HOLIDAY RESORT for Londoners. Its history as a resort dates back to the early 19th century when the villages of Eastwood, Leigh, Prittlewell, Shoebury and Southchurch started to expand along the shores of the Thames estuary. Today, it is also home for thousands of commuters who work in London. Southend pier, almost 2.5km (1.5 miles) long, is the longest in the world and was put to use in the Second World War when 3,367 convoys and 84,297 ships sailed from here.

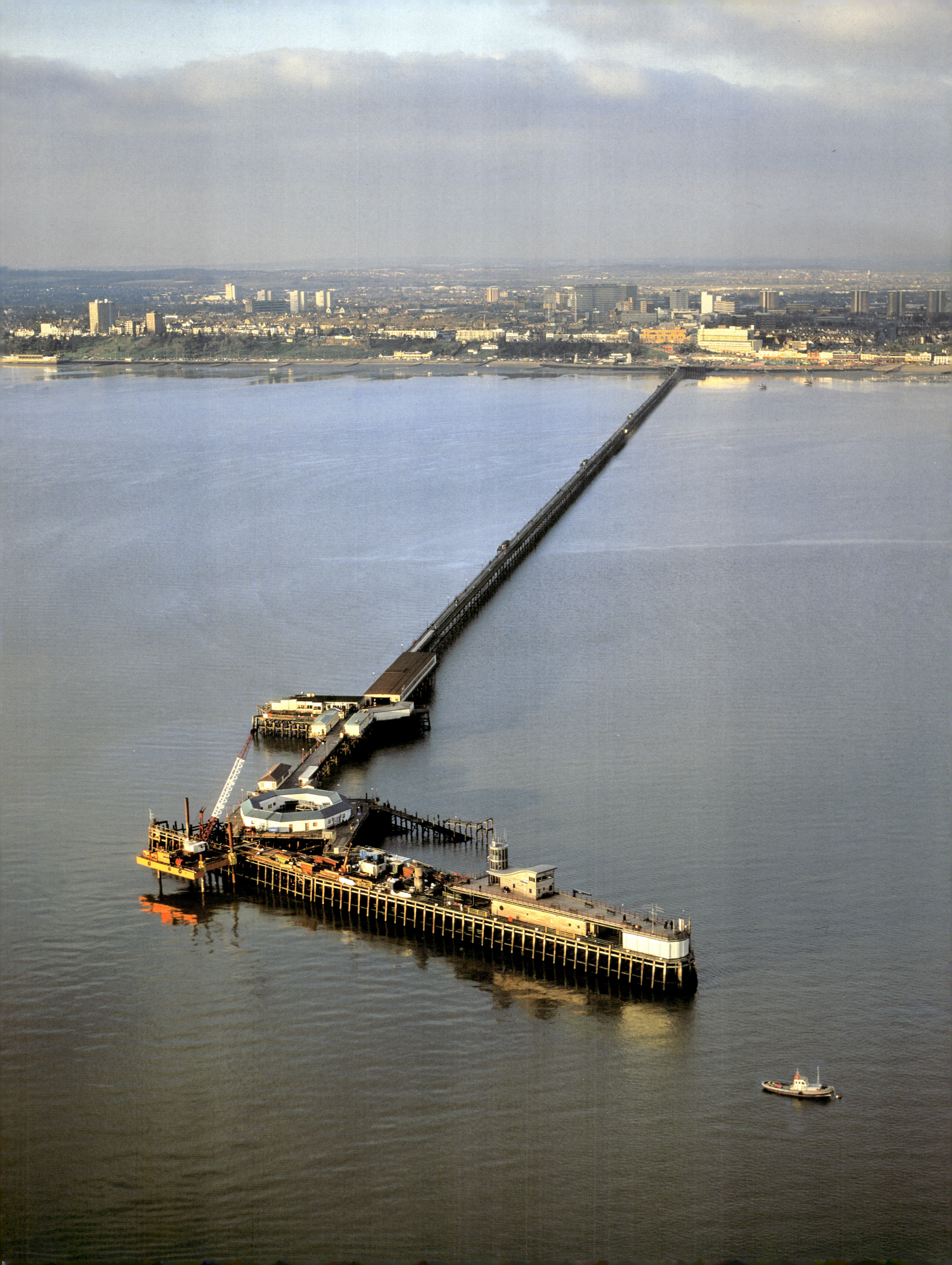

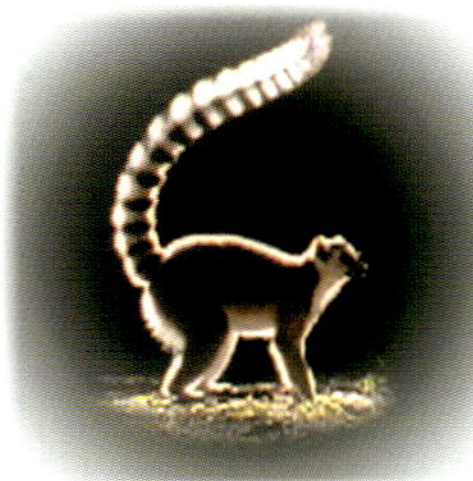

LAST REFUGE Ltd

Nature is a precious inheritance, to be cared for and cherished by all of us. Last Refuge Ltd is a small company primarily dedicated to documenting and archiving endangered environments and species in our rapidly changing world, through films, images and research. The company was established in 1992 for a study of wild giant pandas in the Qinling mountains of central China, which seemed, literally, to be the "last refuge" for these charismatic animals. The company continued to embrace new projects worldwide. Two films on lemurs in Madagascar quickly followed and the ring-tailed lemur became the company's logo. Adrian Warren and Dae Sasitorn, who run the company from a farmhouse in Somerset, have created a special website, www.lastrefuge.co.uk, in order to present their work. This is becoming a huge resource for information, and an extensive photographic archive of still and moving images for both education and media. Ultimately they hope to offer special conservation awards to fund work by others.

ADRIAN WARREN

Adrian Warren is a biologist and a commercial pilot, with over 30 years' experience as a photographer and filmmaker. He has worked worldwide for the BBC Natural History Unit, and as a director in the IMAX giant screen format. He has recently designed a new wing-mounted camera system for aircraft to further develop his interest in aviation, aerial filming and photography. As a stills photographer, he has a personal photographic archive of over 100,000 pictures, with worldwide coverage of wildlife, landscapes, aerials, and peoples. His photographs appear in books, magazines, advertisements, posters, calendars, greetings cards and many other products. His awards include a Winston Churchill Fellowship; the Cherry Kearton Medal from the Royal Geographical Society in London; the Genesis award from the Ark Trust for Conservation; an International Prime Time Emmy; and the Golden Eagle Award from New York.

DAE SASITORN

Dae Sasitorn is an academic from the world of chemistry but has given it up to follow her love for the natural world. She manages the company and is a computer expert. She has created, designed and manages the Last Refuge website as well as scanning thousands of images for the archive. She is also a first-class photographer in her own right.

THE PHOTOGRAPHY

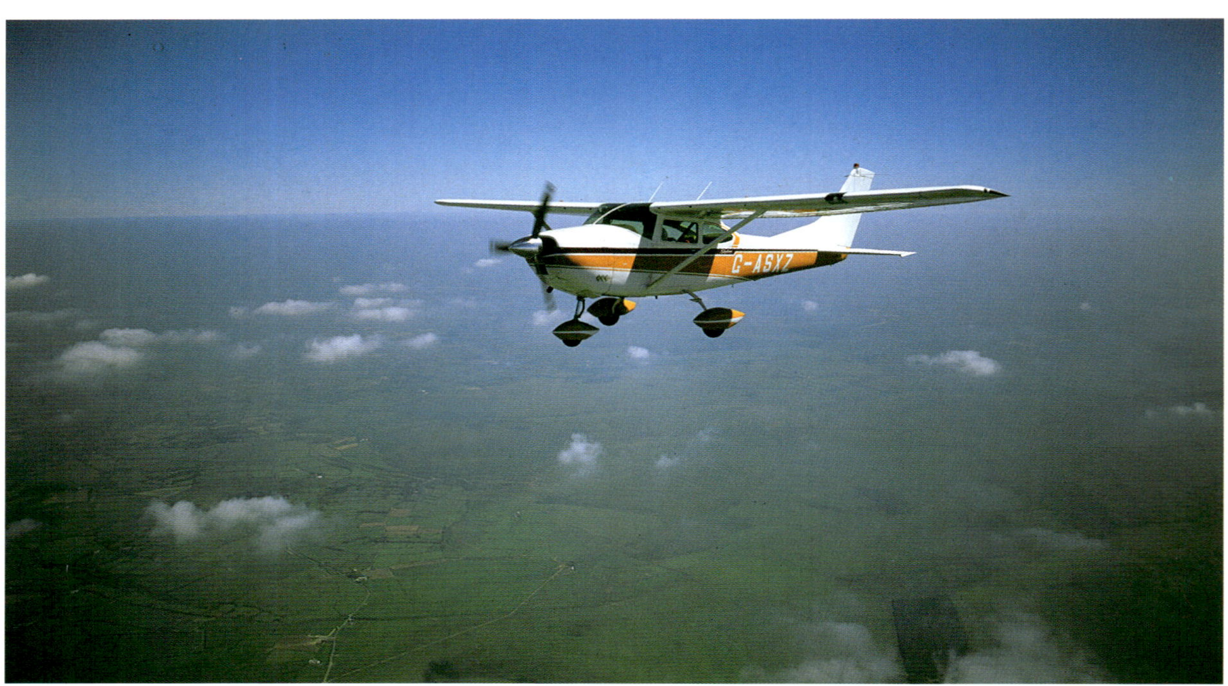

Adrian and Dae operate their own Cessna 182G out of a tiny farm strip close to their house. They bought the single engined four-seater aircraft in May 1999 in order to develop a new wing-mounted camera system for cinematography. The 1964 Cessna was in beautiful condition, and had only one previous owner. It is the perfect aircraft for aerial work: small, manoeuvrable, with plenty of power, and the high wing configuration offering an almost unrestricted view on the world below. With 20 degrees of flap it is possible to fly as slowly as 60 knots. The cabin side window opens upwards and outwards and is kept open by the airflow. The photographs were taken on Hasselblad medium format 6 × 6 cm cameras and lenses using Fujichrome Velvia film. Waiting for the right weather, with a clear atmosphere and less than 50 per cent cloud cover, required being on standby for months.

First Published in 2004 by Myriad Books Limited,
35 Bishopsthorpe Road, London, SE26

ISBN 1 904154 84 0

Designed by Dae Sasitorn and Adrian Warren
Last Refuge Limited
Printed in China